C000146418

SALES IS A VERB
ACTION IS REQUIRED

WHEN MONEY IS ON THE TABLE,
DO YOU KNOW HOW TO EARN IT?

THE STRAIGHT SKINNY FOR
OUTSIDE SALESPEOPLE AND SALES MANAGERS

SONNY CULVER

authorHOUSE®

AuthorHouse™
1663 Liberty Drive
Bloomington, IN 47403
www.authorhouse.com
Phone: 833-262-8899

© 2021 Sonny Culver. All rights reserved.

No part of this book may be reproduced, stored in a retrieval system, or transmitted by any means without the written permission of the author.

Published by AuthorHouse 04/21/2021

ISBN: 978-1-6655-2150-5 (sc)
ISBN: 978-1-6655-2148-2 (hc)
ISBN: 978-1-6655-2149-9 (e)

Library of Congress Control Number: 2021906657

Print information available on the last page.

Any people depicted in stock imagery provided by Getty Images are models, and such images are being used for illustrative purposes only.
Certain stock imagery © Getty Images.

This book is printed on acid-free paper.

Because of the dynamic nature of the Internet, any web addresses or links contained in this book may have changed since publication and may no longer be valid. The views expressed in this work are solely those of the author and do not necessarily reflect the views of the publisher, and the publisher hereby disclaims any responsibility for them.

CONTENTS

FOREWORD

. . . . .

During my sales career I served in Sales, Sales Management, Manager and Region Sales Manager and some time on the Presidents staff. Although I enjoy training people for success, I prefer to lead in the field, where the excitement lives, rather than teach in the corporate training structure. I am not a motivational speaker commanding dopamine and adrenalin or both into my audience. To the contrary I am soft spoken and like most of you, he had a little halfhearted training by someone poorly equipped to train. At some point I realized the act of sales, like handmade furniture is a craft that requires skill and knowledge, and that sellers must be trained and supported in order to become Craftsmen. By using the Craftsman approach, I could build teams of outside sellers who knew how to win and to feel good about their own achievements because they did it the right way.

I accepted a Sales Managers position in an average office with three sellers, one average and two below average, I then added five more. The annual sales budget was $187, 000, five years later the second quarter budget was over $500,000. On the service side there were eight routes running below full capacity. During that same five-year period, we added fourteen routes for a total of twenty-two service routes running at full capacity. That office was now a multimillion-dollar operation.

I left the company for a short time but returned to manage a much smaller branch in a nearby city with no sellers in the office. I hired four good people and the following seven out of twelve month we beat the larger branch in sales. After the manager from an office that was also in a nearby city retired, I assumed management of that office in addition to my current responsibilities. I added two sellers to bring the number to four. During April of that year, which is usually the largest sales month in the pest exterminating business, the larger office sold $225,000 and set a record for that office. My two branches with the same number of sellers (8) but receiving only one half the total number of leads managed twice the closing percentage and sold $226,000. I am pretty damned proud of that.

Whether you are in a small office or a large office and regardless of your product, the principles of Sales is a Verb, Action is Required strategy are very effective in raising sales revenue and an excellent income for the seller.

ACKNOWLEDGEMENTS

* * * * *

"The instruction we find in books is like fire. We fetch it from our neighbors, kindle it at home, communicate it to others, and it becomes the property of all." Voltaire, French writer

* * * * *

Kathryn for the good years and two great kids.

Gloria for encouraging me to write, then listening, reading and editing.

Steve Hullander for your leadership and for being more brother than friend.

Gene Kite for being my mentor when I needed mentoring.

Clyde Cobb for caring enough to lend a helping hand.

PREFACE

● ● ● ● ●

"Entrepreneurship is the last refuge of the troublemaking individual"
James K. Glassman, American Journalist and Businessman

● ● ● ● ●

These pages are about failure and the success it provided. The failure of training, communication and a failure of management and trainers to apply themselves in such a way as to prepare salespeople to be successful. It is also about trial and error and a winning system that is unfailing when followed. Here, we are talking to the salesperson who is knocking on doors and making cold calls and about how to find prospects, making presentations in homes and offices and most emphatically how they can close sales with the customer's confidence. Of no less importance to salespeople is earning a great living and having fun while doing it.

When I graduated high school there were very few jobs that I was qualified for in my hometown. I came from a large family and there was no money for college, so the military was my best option. After serving three years in the US Army I arrived home older but with no applicable skills for employment. Through an employment agency I secured an interview and employment as a manager trainee with a regional cafeteria chain. It was a good job and the training was an intense hands on program. I was assigned to operations in various cities for weeks or months covering vacancies or vacations. Along the way I met the woman who would be my wife until her passing forty-three years later. Suddenly I needed more money, who knew? I moved on to coffee shop operations and did well there. I seized other opportunities until I was able to purchase a national fast food franchise with the ability to grow some personal wealth. I later sold that franchise and did some consultant work, but the downside was that I was away from my family for extended periods of time. That is not the way to go if you want to keep your family no matter how much money you can make.

Looking through the want ads for employment I spied a blind ad. I thought it was probably scam but at the bottom of the ad was, "we will match the salary you are making now." I was negotiating a new consultant contract but thought what the heck. So, I sent a resume and cover letter to the PO Box.

A few days later I received a call from a man saying he was the Region Service Manager form an International Pest Control Company concerning my application for employment. Shortly, I interviewed with the Region Manager and then with the Division Vice President. I was impressed with both men and the RM and I have lasting close friendship. The DVP was hard to read but I remember he asked what I knew about sales. My answer was that my subdivision had a neighborhood yard sale the past weekend. My neighbors sat in lawn chairs and seemed to sell very little but that when someone came to my driveway I would stand and talk to them and that I sold everything but the wife's tables. He said I knew enough, and I was then sent to meet an Industrial Psychologist. It was an interesting interview that took most of a day, but I was recommended for employment. At this point in life I was financially stable, had no fear of hours or hard work and so I became a forty-year-old Manager Trainee. For the record they did not match my income.

My training assignment was to a Branch Office with an experienced manager and office staff some twenty miles from my home. I worked with various service people performing treatment to homes for termites, moisture issues, wood infesting beetles and those occasional invaders no one wants. The service training lasted about a month and then I was assigned to work with the three sellers to learn the sales method. The only one of them who had even a clue what that method was or how it worked was a particularly cantankerous and much older man. Even so, Gene was a tremendous help to me as things soon developed, he became my mentor.

Some six weeks into training I was invited to attend a Managers Meeting and to be introduced to Managers from around the Region.

The meeting started with posting the board for the previous days sales, all meetings I attended started with and ended with sales momentum. At noon the RM was called away for a phone call and shortly afterwards my training manager left the meeting. There had been a serious infraction of policy and his employment was terminated. I arrived early to the branch office the following morning and went to the front office to see if there were any task that needed attention. I was given a request for a home inspection and directions to a bank to get the house key. There were active termites in the house and the garage. Not knowing any better I filled in a contract for service and took it to the bank manager who signed it and issued a check to my company. In the parking lot a man stopped me and asked if I did inspections, I told him that I did and being a right now personality I went with him to his home. There was no infestation of any kind, but he wanted the home treated for termites and monthly service for pest. After the paperwork was done, he said he wanted me to meet his neighbor and we walked across both yards. After introductions and an inspection, I wrote my fourth contract for the day. It was late afternoon when I arrived at the branch office and was met immediately by the RM who rather gruffly asked where had I been? I explained how the day started and handed him four contracts all meeting the rate card for sales. I understood his situation well because I had had multi-unit responsibility over multiple states and knew exactly what he was experiencing. He paced up and down the long hallway at a rapid pace, as I learned was his thinking habit, and after a few minutes he came to me and said; "I am placing you as manager of this office effective today". The day after that when I looked around my new office, I found training tapes and workbooks that I had not been exposed to, I took them home to train myself after hours. My nearly twenty years working in the exterminating industry was in six different branch offices and a year on the Presidents staff and as a Region Sales Manager. For the most part the Pest Exterminating business is the best job anyone could dream of having and some days were so much fun that I would have worked for free and that is the truth. After retirement I wanted to test myself with an eye on writing this book and so for several companies, I was either a salesman or sales manager. In home sales for roofing, siding, windows, and fencing and insurance with a record of success in each and every product. Today I buy and sell houses, apartments and commercial property; some call it flipping real estate.

What follows are the lessons I learned about prospecting, closing sales, and what was important about recruiting the most likely people to be successful and how to train them to become a Craftsman in sales. I present to you a simple but well-developed system that turned huge revenue dollars in multiple markets. Absorb it and have fun making money because you can do it.

BUILDING YOURSELF AND YOUR SALESMANSHIP INTO A CRAFT

YOUR PERSONAL BRAND

● ● ● ● ●

"Branding is what people say about you
when you are not in the room."
Jeff Bezos, Founder and CEO Amazon.com

● ● ● ● ●

We see entertainers and products that are immediately recognizable because of their brand. Coca Cola, BMW and Apple are a few of the most notable brands in our lives and yet they are timeless. Brands are designed and promoted to have a personal and bonding relationship with you. Your personal brand is about managing your name in a complex world to build bonding relationships that lead to prospects and customers. Your brand is a voice that speaks for your professional knowledge, expectations met, memories of trust and likability, stories and relationships. It identifies you by your appearance, demeanor and professionalism and also by how you treat coworkers and your online persona. These are the necessary tools to influence the consumer's decision to choose you as their vendor. Your personal brand is too important for you not have total control of it, and it should be so distinctly different that no competitor can match you.

For management your personal brand will extend to how you treat the people in your charge, how well you manage people both up and down line. Communication happens on many levels, but verbal is often the least effective unless it is negative which leads to a negative response. Negative communication is always personal.

1

If you are an experienced seller you already have a personal brand, how well does it work for you, does it open doors for appointments and referrals? Without thinking state your personal brand as a statement of value and do it aloud right now. If you paused or had to think or if what you just said was longer than two sentences or twenty seconds and wasn't based in building relationships, you have some more work to do. Your personal brand must be courageous enough not to lie, adaptive enough not to become rigid and flexible enough to deliver a comprehensive package that meets customer approval and gets referrals. You must have adaptive behavior because the last thing you expect in this disruptive age is certain to happen, Murphy is always lurking in the shadows. Your personal brand is about selling you and therefore it must have a certainty about it that creates trust and the necessary cooperation from others to build relationships with total strangers. That doesn't mean you have to be all things to all people, that is unsustainable and a competitive disadvantage for you, plus it's impossible. Being trusted is the most powerful emotion in business and it is also the best brand strategy for a salesperson. It really does matter what people think of you because you need them bonded to you and to be dedicated to your business on a deep level. Perception is reality in the eye of the prospect.

Your personal brand is not about product, it is about attracting prospects, customers and referrals through your ability to form relationships. Your personal brand is designed to set you apart from your competitors, and it should tell your prospects that you are the person they want to deal with no matter the product. In order to communicate your brand, you will need a statement of value that describes you, will hold the prospects attention, will cause prospects to want to know more and that will open the door for appointments and referrals. Make your Brand Statement interesting but not more than two sentences and ten to twenty seconds in length, after all you are a professional seller but not a shameless self-promoter. No one will ever know who you are unless you can tell your prospect in a compelling way what you do and why you do it and what the positive impact is for them, otherwise your expertise, knowledge, skill and ability will be a well-kept secret. Do it well and word will spread quickly because when people have something interesting to talk about, they want to tell it again and again. Work on your personal brand until you are a Craftsman in Sales and you no longer have to introduce yourself.

Before you can build a robust statement of value to communicate your personal brand you will need to understand yourself. It makes good since to look as critically at yourself as you would someone else and it's probably not going to be easy, but it is necessary. I am certainly not your analyst, but there can are a few tips and questions that you can use to help define yourself and be more effective in management and more successful in sales. What is your brand and how is it identified?

How well do you understand yourself, and your social connections?

Are your goals well defined?
Are you known to be emotional, can you accept imperfection?
Are you proud or humble?
Can you confront your own unproductive emotions and responses?
Is your self-awareness as acute as your awareness of other people's faults?
Are your actions or reactions productive for building relationships?
Are you trusted in your workplace and in social groups?
Who are you?
What do you do?
Why should the prospect do business with you?
What makes you different?
Are you trustworthy?
How can you help the prospect?
What do you want your target prospects to know about your services?
What do you want to be known for?
What is your mission statement?
Do you think before responding?

Start now, be honest and specific, write down everything that you can think of about yourself and what is truly unique to you, your accomplishments and licensing level, your company and why you are the best value with whom to do business. Define your interest, awards, benchmarks, goals reached, hobbies and your background because these things define you, but no jargon. Avoid describing yourself as a salesman or a Territory Manager because that information is time consuming and offers no value for the prospect. Articulate the value the prospect will receive from you, not just the mechanics of the task itself.

Don't just think about it write it down, the more the better, there is no wrong and you can edit later after you finish brainstorming. Input from people who are close to you may be helpful, but you must be open minded. Edit and rewrite until you have worked it down to an acceptable two sentences ranging from ten to twenty seconds length and time. Now take out that dreaded digital recorder and practice your statement of value until you can't do it wrong. More editing will be necessary, but you are a professional seller on your way to becoming a Craftsman, what else do you have to do? Most people will have good intentions or even be motivated at this point, but you have to own it, good intentions won't buy a cup of coffee if you can't make positive connections that lead to appointments, closed deals and referrals.

A bit of marketing is necessary on your part to inform the community that you are a reliable, trustworthy and respected seller who comes to mind when your product or service is in demand. You should obtain membership in organizations that represent credibility and reliability to consumers who are shopping for professionals. Join civic organizations and the Better Business Bureau and your local Chamber of Commerce. These organizations give you a third-party credibility, something potential clients often find more convincing than your sales presentation. Be prepared to have your prospects call the BBB, the Chamber of Commerce and client testimonials that highlight your ability to create solutions, encourage them to do so. After joining these organizations, it will be helpful to volunteer on committees and/or projects that agree with your personal values or beliefs, especially true at your place of worship.

When you are able be sure to donate your time and money. You will also want to attend meetings, mixers and fundraising events. On your website post photos and list your memberships and the events, event planning and projects where you have contributed time and don't forget about your family photos. Let other business professionals know who you are, and let them know they can confidently refer their friends and clients to you, but you had better thoroughly know your business, know your target market and know everything you can learn about the target prospects business.

**"You can use all the right words in marketing,
but it doesn't matter if people
have no interest in reading them. Branding trumps copy –
don't underestimate the power of your visual brand."
Re Perez, CEO and founder Branding for People**

DEVELOPING SUCCESS SKILLS

● ● ● ● ●

Destiny is no matter of chance. It is a matter of choice.
It is not a thing to be waited for; it is a thing to be achieved.
William Jennings Bryan, American Lawyer and Politician

● ● ● ● ●

READING PROSPECTS, ASSOCIATES and the BOSS
D.I.S.C. - Dominance - Influencing - Steadiness - Conforming
SOCIAL STYLES – Analytical – Driver – Amiable - Expressive

Know who you are by understanding your personality and the personalities of those around you. Combine your Social Style and D.I.S.C. self-analysis with your Personal Brand building and it will pay off in big ways for you by being able to better read and anticipate prospects and associate behavior. Understanding the prospects personality, their weaknesses, strengths, birth order and the best way to present and close to each personality type is of great value to you. Hint, whatever you are at work will change in your family setting, there is a test for that too.

For management it stands to reason that before you modify your own behavior, much less help other people adapt to successful behavior, you will need to understand your own individual Social Style and D.I.S.C. scores. We may not be consciously aware of certain of our behavioral traits, whether or not they are productive, but we know exactly how we treat other people. The first step is to be willing to change if there is a need to and then be sure you get noticed but in a way that compliments your personality and your Sales Craftsmanship.

The first time I took this exercise my Dominance was off the grid, the last time I took it Dominance was my next to the lowest on the scale and my Influencing (social affiliation) was the highest with Steadiness (relationship) close by while Conforming (fear and uncertainty) was the lowest. What happened, maturity for sure, but more so being comfortable in my capabilities. In that process my emotional drive changed from aggressiveness to social affiliation. My Social Style is Driver with strong leanings toward analytical, imagine bringing a lame activity report or sloppy paperwork to that guy.

MOTIVATION: Sales is a multifaceted Craft and we can learn something from any motivational speaker, but we cannot depend upon them for success. Motivation may be the spark that gets you going, but it is establishing good habits that will make you successful. Motivation is an emotional response; the Craftsman must depend upon his or her ability to think in terms of strategy. Every action and reaction you take has an end result for which you have responsibility. The Craftsman's motivation starts by expecting to win because they prepare a plan to win, it ends with nice commission checks.

Some people simply cannot be motivated to do anything productive or creative, to be blunt, they have lazy brains, or their nature is so negative that they take pleasure in the failure of others, even when their own income is affected. Remove them from association with active sellers or they will poison the team and kill productivity.

Your assignment is to learn the steps to Craftsmanship that cause your clients to depend upon you, how to make people comfortable telling you their problems. To learn the social styles of people and the unique circumstances of each that you will need to know while presenting to different personalities and in different situations. Start now.

HOPE: Hope is not a motivator; it is a de-motivator, but there is a place for the strength of hope when fortified with goals and a well-planned strategy. Hope without strategy is only a wish. Vince Lombardi, a great motivator and winning coach said, "Hope is not a strategy." We can hope our favorite sports teams win or that we win the lottery or for world peace. We can hope for these things and others, but we have no control over them. If you will view Sales as a Craft and practice your Craft to perfection, as a Craftsman who builds fine furniture would, hope for success will not be necessary. Politicians speak of hope, because they want you to vote for them and send your money so that you will have hope. Most of them have sold their souls to make you feel the victim of oppression by all those more powerful than you. Guess what, the politicians do not need hope because they have a strategy fueled by the knowledge of where they want to go and how they are going to build their careers. Their minds are actively prospecting and networking for money, votes, and power, methods similar to those used by Craftsman salespeople. If a salesperson knows what he or she wants and is not afraid to invest the mental energy needed to learn how to sell, and of equal importance, how to read the prospect, then the seller will not need external motivation much less clinging desperately to wishful hope.

RULE OF THUMB: "Whatever got you to where you are today is not enough to get you any further." What this means is that your current level of knowledge and skill has been sufficient to achieve your current income and standard of living. But in order for you to improve, to move onward and upward, you must learn and apply new skills essential for professional and personal growth. And there is no other way to get ahead except to become better at what you do, your best game will become your current standard. Raise the stakes and reach further, success is there for the taking.

RULE OF THUMB: "For life to get better, *you* must get better." The good news is that there are no limits to how much better you can become. Therefore, there are no limits to how much more you can change your life if you have the determination and the discipline to do so. Every day in every way you should be looking for ways to change your life for the better and increase your performance. Time cannot change anything, only your mindset and the dedication to your work can do that.

PERSISTENCE & DETERMINATION: "Nothing in the world can take the place of persistence. Talent will not; nothing is more common than unsuccessful men with talent. Genius will not; unrewarded genius is almost a proverb. Education will not; the world is full of educated derelicts. Persistence and determination alone are omnipotent." President Calvin Coolidge had the right idea, we have all known people who had talent, intelligence, and education, yet never succeeded in business or in life? Why didn't they succeed? Attitude! Yes, you've heard it many times before, but I'll say it again. It comes down to attitude and your resulting behavior. An attitude of persistence and determination can more than make up for what you lack in talent or education. Attitude is the driving force that helps to create success. If you have the persistence and determination to succeed, you will succeed!

SUCCESS: Success changes circumstances and it changes people. Dealing with success is more difficult than dealing with failure. Successful people are expected continue at a level of high-performance and improve upon production with no end point for more and greater things. After all, isn't the bounty just waiting in plain sight for the successful? Those who are less than successful can and probably will place blame where they think it will stick but will rarely take responsibility for their own failure. Success has many fathers, but failure is an orphan. If you want more success you must acknowledge it and accept it, failing to accept your success is a method of avoiding success. Never accept failure, just find another strategy.

Peers, associates and even family may become envious of your success, but you cannot control the reactions of others. What you can do is spread the credit for success. Some will think you are unapproachable and avoid you even as you mentor to them for their success. If those things cause you to feel guilty about your success, you are normal. Your best reaction is to acknowledge your success if you want more of it, otherwise you are avoiding success and the edge will disappear. It is OK to celebrate a little, but the humble person will be more admired and respected.

SELF DISCIPLINE: There are the lucky few who have perfect bone structure or are always at the right place and at the precisely right time. The rest of us must apply self-disciplined thought and actions along with hard work to reach our goals. However, if the desire to achieve truly exists in your heart and soul you can shape yourself, your character and your career in the most positive ways. No one has said it will be easy, you will need self-attention, intention and the will to overcome a few setbacks, difficulties and resistance from within and without. We must observe ourselves as we progress. The good news is that as you strengthen one discipline others are strengthened and complement one another and your confidence will soar.

Visualize situations past present or future and then see yourself succeed. You are standing on the mound of your favorite baseball team. It is the bottom of the ninth inning and bases are loaded; the score is 3 to 2 in your favor. There are two outs, and the count is three balls and two strikes with a .300 hitter at the plate, history rest heavily on your shoulders. The catcher gives the signal, but you shake it off. The manager is signaling with every limb of his body. Here's what you do, visualize a ninety-five mile per hour fast ball and focus on the catcher's mitt in the middle of the strike zone. Wind up, turn it loose and watch it through. What happens next doesn't matter and is out of your control, but your focus, positive self-affirmation and self-discipline put you in the position to win. Any way you cut that up you are a winner.

LISTENING: Far too many sellers would rather talk than listen and earnestly believe sales is a contest of wills. That if they talk longer or louder or fast enough the sale will close and yet he (has hope) that it will. It won't, and that seller won't get far in business without building and maintaining relationships.

A successful career in sales requires many skills but none are more important than to be an active, attentive and disciplined listener. You must learn to listen with your eyes and your ears. People reveal a great deal with their body language when they talk. Feel the emotion in what your prospect is telling you and the underlying buying signals displayed.

Take careful notes, no one can retain every point made by the prospect and the one you miss may be the most important.

Sellers with a false since of confidence are often judgmental, aloof and enjoy stereotyping or pre-judging the prospect. For them the final results of the sale in front of them has already been decided, and it is lost. Whereas the seller who can listen, is non-judgmental, neutral, unassuming and confident will have the prospects attention and a signature on the contract.

REFERENCE:

D.I.S.C. personality test – William Moulton Marston, Phycologist
Social Styles – David Merrill & Roger Reid

"Income seldom exceeds personal improvement."
Jim Rohn, American Entrepreneur, Author and Motivational Speaker

ETHICS FOR SALESPEOPLE

● ● ● ● ●

"Ethics is not about definitions...It's about the inner impulses,
judgments, and duties of people like you and me."
Rushworth Kidder, author of How Good People Make Tough Choices

● ● ● ● ●

Ethics are about obeying The Golden Rule, do that and you can never go wrong. The power of Ethics is not having to choose between right and wrong. Honoring Ethics in Sales can be defined as delivering a customer experience that lives up to the highest standards of contribution to service and community no matter how great or small. Ethics require courage to do the right thing when others do not. Ethics require respect, integrity and with honesty and is the highest form of respect. Ethics require servanthood, it is a greater honor to serve than to be served. Serving others is a personalized approach to the customer and fosters a positive experience at all transaction points.

For our purpose we are talking about Ethics as a part of Sales as a Craft. Think of Sales Ethics as your credibility kit. Knowing, behaving and deciding are the key factors of maintaining the highest personal standards of Ethics for sellers. If you want to be a top seller the highest standard of Sales Ethics is absolutely mandatory for you. Let's identify some of those areas we need to develop for perfection.

Be accountable and always fully disclose and explain information in language that the prospect will understand and that means no jargon, in order for the prospect to make the best buying decision. The prospect should have questions about your products and services, but if they do not, you must educate them anyway. Never skip over or misrepresent facts to close a sale, but always serve your prospects best interest.

Never pressure a prospect to buy using fear, that is a bullying technique, it is not a tactic. Contracts signed using fear will cancel as soon as you leave the prospect's home or business. You lose the sale, credibility and referrals, plus you worked free.

Be the person you are, some people use words to select who they want to be, but actions always show who they really are. Be humble and honest about who you are and be shy about any awards or designations you hold. Phony sellers work harder and sell less.

Learn to be a great communicator; you will never fix a problem if you can't identify it. Practice using your digital voice recorder to ask and answer questions. Ask your customers how they feel about your products or services and fix anything they aren't happy with and do it now.

Build value and trust by accepting accountability for what is understood as well as what is heard. People like and appreciate sellers who are helpful and kind but not the pushy person. When you build trust you also get recommendations from people describing your professional expertise. When people trust that you will behave in a professional way you get introductions and referrals. Your success will be the consequence of your behavior.

Trust can be transferred from one person to another when a relationship has been formed. Once you have earned someone's trust, ask him or her for introductions, they will want to help you. Trust is one of the most productive networking actions sellers can take. But it can also work in the reverse: trust and your reputation can be damaged very quickly if there is a hint of lying or dishonesty. Never lie about your company's capabilities or hide its pricing from your prospects, they will choose another seller and share that you are not trustworthy with their friends. People profoundly distrust those who mislead them. What people remember is how you handle mistakes and errors, not what the situation was. Be reliable and do what you say you will do, and a little more. Knowing someone personally and showing interest in them goes a long way toward building trust.

Craftsman know that customers prefer honest salespeople and will bring repeat business and referrals to the seller. It's the average or under performer who does not understand that honesty sells. Those are the salespeople who may have a complicated relationship with the truth because they are fear driven liars. It's not hard to understand why because we have all been in that situation. After a week or two of poor detail being given to our training by someone who just wants to get it over with, we are given a sales kit and told to go sell. Too bad for us, right. Fear driven liars are compromised when they tweak facts to improve the odds closing a sale; truth is more practical than lying. Honesty is a more persuasive tactic plus it attracts future business.

This part is very important to you, success is not a goal, it is a byproduct of doing good things for other people.

"Be a yardstick of quality.
Some people aren't used to an environment
where excellence is expected."
Steve Jobs, founder of Apple Corporation

ACCOUNTABILITY

● ● ● ● ●

"It is not only what we do, but also what we do not do
for which we are accountable".
John Baptiste Molière, French play write, actor and poet

● ● ● ● ●

Take pride in your accountability. The expectation level does not decrease and should increase as experience and training reinforce ability. Personal accountability requires mindfulness, acceptance, honesty and courage. The absence of personal accountability is disrespectful to one's self and to others.

In an interview with a Vice President I was more told than asked, "You're not a natural salesman are you". To be honest I was not a natural salesman and I proudly continue not to be, but I am successful on the never-ending path to Craftsmanship. I had recently been transferred to an office that had been poorly operated over an extended period of time, the staff was hostile to customers and management and I was struggling to run the business because the volume of serious daily customer complaints was staggering. To add to those issues my new Region Manager was having a fling with my incompetent office manager, both married of course. The VP was known to harshly criticize and demand a very high, often unreasonable, standard of performance, all accountability was downhill. The customer service company that the three of us worked for was ignoring accountability to the customer, that accountability was set-aside because he wanted to look good and sales came first no matter what. Both men were a fraud because leaders inspire accountability through their ability to accept responsibility before they place blame. The VP's accountability came when he was fired for mishandling his people. He was so hated that throughout the Division that there were office parties to celebrate his dismissal. Accountability is a two-way street, what goes down must come back up. Accountability is the glue that ties commitment to results.

Do you look reality directly in the face and deny it? I know you do; we have all done that, but you don't have to. Here is a short list of lies salespeople tell themselves and their bosses to avoid accountability and the success that affects corporate and personal earnings.

I can't reach my quota because the price is too high: Price is always a factor in every sale, but it is seldom the primary reason people make their final buying decision. Very few companies will set their pricing higher than the target market will bear. If you rely solely on price failing to establish value to close deals you are not a salesperson, you are just an order taker.

I've got this deal pending: No, you don't. This is probably the most common lie for salespeople to tell. That big deal is good when it falls but they rarely close and if all of your fish are in one hand it will be a lean payday. Prospects on large deals will often tell you everything you want to hear, usually to get rid of you, only to balk at making a final decision. They were not going to buy, and they knew it, suspects are liars, not prospects and buyers. No deal is guaranteed until the prospect signs the contract and service is scheduled or a delivery date is confirmed. A supervisor should accompany any but the most experienced salesperson for larger deals.

The competition has cheaper prices: Of course, they do, if price is all they have. Loan sharks and bankers sell money; sales Craftsman sell products and services fortified by real and perceived value. We were the highest priced company in our field but we literally reaped volumes of business from cheaper priced companies.

I don't need to set a sales commitment: If you truly feel that way, I am hopeful your spouse has a really good job because you are dying on the vine. Some companies do not require sales goals but that is sloppy business, after all no one can monitor performance without tracking results. We met individually and as a group six days each week to post the board and talk about sales and experiences, on Mondays there was a training meeting. On the first day of each month I posted the sales budget on the leader board and each sale person posted his/her commitment for the month. They never posted a total less than the budgeted amount. Make it clear that commitments are in blood and if you give me a contract and it later councils, you owe me the make-up. Craftsmen always set ambitious sales goals, and their target goals are usually higher than those set by their companies. They use these goals to inspire and motivate themselves to achieve more. A top selling sales manager must require a sales goal commitment.

No one is buying: Regardless of the economy, people and companies still make buying decisions and spend money for products and services. Don't waste time thinking about the people who aren't buying and go find the people and companies who are buying. Good marketing, prospecting and personal branding are the remedy when the economy dips. Take a breath, the Capitalist System always recovers.

No one buys during the holidays: People are conditioned to spend large amounts of money during the Holidays, all you have to do is ask.

I don't need to practice my sales presentation: Everyone needs to practice not only his or her presentation but warm up close and cool down as well. In my offices it was mandatory to possess a digital recorder for rehearsal and practice. Managers often instruct a new salesperson to learn the presentation and practice on the spouse. He or she has no idea what they are hearing but will tell you how great you did it. You could present to your dog, but he will be bored to curl up and go to sleep. You and you only know how the presentation should sound and the digital recorder will quickly point out mistakes and where you need to emphasize more or less. Top sellers seldom take their sales appointments and meetings for granted. They rehearse the questions they need to ask. They run through their presentations to make sure they have included the necessary details and that their presentations flow in a logical manner and address their prospects situation and/or needs. This part is very important to you, use a digital recorder or even better do it on camera and prepare yourself for success. Practice until you can't do it wrong.

As a Region Sales Manager I would visit offices across the state, on one of these visits the manager was holding a sales meeting and a struggling seller was giving his presentation. Every excuse imaginable for his failure was on the table and none were his fault. When we played back the recording he had said, "you know," forty-seven times. You know, that was a terrible presentation but with practice and a digital recorder he became a productive member of his sales team and so can you. Whoever first said practice makes perfect but perfect practice makes winners was absolutely right, but I say practice until you can't get it wrong.

The Green Bay Packers under coach Vince Lombardi won the first two Super Bowls. The Packer sweep, student body left, was their most powerful play. Everyone knew they were going to run it, but no one could stop it. The simple reason why is that starting with wind sprints and virtually everything done in practice was from that formation including the last thing done at the end of practice, it was perfect practice. If you are still a nonbeliever for perfect practice, just watch a Dabo Swinney or Nick Saban football team on the field, you will see perfect practice in action.

ACCOUNTABILITY TO THE CUSTOMER: What if we had a written set of Accountability Principles, and shared it with our customers, telling them what they could expect from the seller and his company. We could express our loyalty and assure the customer we would keep in the strictest confidence, all business, personal and financial information pertaining to our customers affairs. We could encourage the courtesy of timely notification if service expectations are not met or exceeded. It would be a great trust builder tailored to the customer and open conversation to make sure all expectations are clear. The customer can see that you care about the relationship and how it is to grow. When the customer is happy and satisfied with your service you can expect introductions and referrals without asking.

Responsibility equals accountability equals ownership. And a sense of ownership is the most powerful weapon a team or organization can have.
Pat Summit, Basketball Coach, University of Tennessee

TIME MANAGEMENT

● ● ● ● ●

"Everything requires time. It is the only truly universal condition. All work takes place in time and uses up time. Yet most people take for granted this unique, irreplaceable, and necessary resource. Nothing else, perhaps, distinguishes effective executives as much as their tender loving care of time."
Peter F. Drucker, American author

● ● ● ● ●

We cannot manage time, it moves too quickly for us, but we can manage our thoughts and the resulting activities. Every phase of a successful life requires self-discipline, but self-discipline begins with the mastery of our thoughts and if we do not control our thoughts, we can't control what we do or what happens to us. The choice is yours to make, take control of yourself through your thoughts and actions or others to take control of you, your time, your energy, your money and career.

The experts who tell us how to run our businesses say to prioritize a To Do List with no more than six items, but what if you have a full legal pad with aging corners, someone is at your office door and the phone is ringing. You are busy and distracted but I can promise you that no one will care, they only want what they want, and they expect you to comply. To be more effective shouldn't we start with a prioritized NOT TO DO LIST, you know what should be on it so write it down? After all, isn't it the habits we should not do but do anyway that cause distraction, delayed planning, failure to act, interrupt communications and bring us chaos and stress? To succeed in business, you must be focused and fully committed to your plan and your goals, so dig deep through those layers of clutter or just plain bovine droppings and attend to what matters. What matters is doing what matters and if you are not doing what matters, nothing positive will occur.

Now that you have written your NOT TO DO LIST it is important to move on to productive behavior. You will need to write down the most important projects for today and others on a future calendar date. If you need to react to a change in priorities, and you will, do it because you must remain flexible but be sure to focus on productivity. Your list may have two or ten projects, it doesn't matter how many projects so long as you plan for productivity and know the outcome of each project, now you are in control. When you are in control of the flow, you can move to the offensive and make things happen instead of allowing those things to happen to you. We are all allotted the same amount of time in a day, control implies delegating, organizing and planning skills and the knowledge of your options.

Getting organized is the first step you must take and that means collecting all of your projects and putting them into an order of attack, with an eye on each project for beyond the completion date. Reorganize your office space until it works best for you. Streamline your office for maximum productivity and a minimum of distractions. Protect your privacy to concentrate and discuss issues. For every action there is a reaction so you must plan for that as well.

Effective planning is planning with a specific purpose for the desired outcome of a project or situation but at the same time allowing for the human factor to alter results. Asking yourself why I am doing this and what is the projected time frame for conclusion and what is the projected outcome, is a good question for each action you plan to take. Hope will not help you to plan effectively, you must develop a strategy.

Delegating, for Management, is a major part of keeping yourself organized, and it must be a part of your mission-oriented plan. Be sure to supply the right information to the right person. Tell them what to do, tell them again and tell them to do it along with expected results and a time frame for completion. Be sure to follow up because a project may explode into something bigger and more expensive. Poor delegating leads to mistakes, a breakdown of training and causes employee turnover. Be sure that all lines of authority are clearly defined.

Our interaction with other people consumes a huge portion of our day and if we cannot communicate clearly there will be complications, mistakes and wasted time that we cannot afford to lose. But there are among us arrogant people who actually believe, "if you don't understand what I am telling you it's not my fault." Every employee needs to know what is going on and how he or she and their job fit into the overall picture. Otherwise your employees will have an unclear and a confused picture of how to proceed and so they must assume, often wrongly. Being certain that the person you are speaking with clearly understands every word you speak is your responsibility. In order to achieve that clarity, you must also be an attentive listener and be able ask the right questions. Use your digital recorder to practice until you can speak as smoothly as a politician, without the lies of course. Communicating effectively will establish credibility and a positive image of and for you.

If you will do these things your relationship with God, your career, work life and family life will improve beyond your wildest dreams.

> *The key is in not spending time but investing in it.*
> **Stephen R. Covey** *author of, The 7*
> *Habits of Highly Effective People*

SERVICING THE CUSTOMER

● ● ● ● ●

"There is only one boss: The customer and he can fire everybody in the company from the Chairman on down by simply spending his money somewhere else."
Sam Walton, Founder and Chairman of Wal-Mart

● ● ● ● ●

Service is a duty to someone who has paid you to perform certain duties and actions. The service relationship you develop with your customers will decide your retention rates and revenue capture. It takes time and extra energy from everyone involved to deal with the vicious cycle of unfulfilled promises and dishonesty caused by poor attention to service. When service is not the cornerstone of your business none of the rest will matter because your business won't last long.

If you have never entertained an irate customer at some point in your career you are indeed fortunate. Your first hint of trouble is when the customers opening statement is, "you people." A few people will vent their life or family frustrations upon any defenseless person that can be further punished if they do not yield to the demand to be verbally abused. They will scream at you in a loud voice and may even use profane and colorful euphemisms to describe you and your company. There may be a volume of expletives directed at you and often they will threaten to sue you, your company and your great uncle. An associate answered a call from a woman who had called several times over a period of minutes only to be greeted be a shrill whistle. The associate recoiled, then asked, "what the hell was that" the answer was "it was my rape whistle." We had to have a meeting because of what the associate told her to do with the whistle.

There are some effective ways to deal with angry customers and build positive relationships, but you must remain calm and helpful. Responding is not about stealing thunder; as sales professionals it is about preventing the loss of a customer and the revenue associated with that customer and the associated loss of future business. One of the easiest screamers to handle is the threat to sue. I would answer, "I am so sorry you said that" and then be silent. The customer will always respond by asking "why." Now I am in control answering, "I really want to help you as quickly as I can, but you just took away my ability to speak with you." It never failed to calm the customer and I could arrange a satisfactory result. Other times, because you have no idea of the challenges in the customer's life, you just have to wait until they have vented before you can reestablish communications, often the door will be open for additional sales. It is a very odd human factor, but people will feel obligated to appease after they have abused and insulted someone who is in their service.

I wager that about now you are wondering how this guy can tell me to give excellent service after stating how he didn't, and I am glad you asked that question. I successfully managed several offices and the reward was relocation to a larger office along with an increase in salary and bonus. Only the relatives of executives and the most adept at patronizing the boss will inherit a well-run operation. The rest of have to work. We do not and may never know what is going on in the life of the person who calls in an angry complaint, but we must try to understand.

True story: Generally, we worked half days on Saturday, but I had only been in this office for a few weeks and there was a lot to do. On this particular Saturday I was the only one in the office around six PM when the phone rang. The lady on the other end of the call said, "I am going to blow up your office, do you hear me." As you may guess she had my undivided attention and at the same time noticed my office had no window to the outside. As it turns out her husband had recently lost his life in an accident and the lady was in an upside-down world to say the least, she needed and deserved help. I called home to cancel dinner plans and went to the customers home, confirmed the she had an unaddressed problem and accompanied the service tech on Monday to make a correction. Run down offices can be tough to operate, but the reward on the customers face when you make it right is a tremendous satisfaction.

The only successful way to keep customers happy is to consistently go the extra mile and exceed their expectations. In order to do that there are character traits that must be in place at every level of your company. There are key character traits in you and your associates that determine whether or not satisfactory service can be rendered. Just for the record satisfactory <u>ain't</u> good enough. As you read on think about how your customers would rate your character traits and the quality of service you provide. Would you hire you?

Dependability: When you make a commitment to a customer you must remember to under promise and over deliver. Your word is taken literally, and your customers expect you to live up to your promises. Failing to be dependable will affect your ability to grow your business while you are losing customers.

Respectful: Everyone you meet deserves respect but no one more than your customer and especially those that are difficult to work with or upset. Rudeness or displaying unprofessional behavior is the fastest way to lose a customer for life and perhaps get you fired. Showing honest respect to your customer will gain his or her respect in return.

Proactive: A proactive approach is to identify and resolve customer service issues before they become a problem. You can even solve problems before your clients realizes they exist. Be inventive and show initiative when solving customer complaints. Compliancy kills business and careers.

Positive mental attitude: If you believe that sales is about that wonderful thing about to happen and that service is about that horrible thing that just happened, you are in the wrong job. First impressions are

25

extremely important and there is absolutely no substitute for a cheerful disposition and a helpful attitude. Neglect your customers and they will find someone else to accept their money.

You are in business to attract new customers and keep the ones you have. It makes good business since to develop guidelines that clearly define what good customer service entails and how it is best delivered to create a customer-centric culture in your office. Then empower your employees with policies that allow the employee the power to deliver superlative service.

Always side with the customer.

Inform the customer that you will take up the issue and then do it.

Define to staff how to service customers. Tell them what to do and tell them to do it.

Detail the specifics of each failure and how to prevent a recurrence.

Instill pride in a job well done.

Tell the customer what they will experience and then deliver.

Call your customers and review calls with employees.

Find people with good attitudes and reinforce it every day with non-stop training.

Employees who feel appreciated will always give more than is expected.

Service is a topic of conversation in every office and on every day, but the bottom line is talk doesn't fix service issues, only action will do that.

"I believe in the power of recognition and empowerment leading to a great employee engagement. And employee engagement is critical to guest engagement. Employee empowerment and recognition is the core of our culture *and how we achieve outstanding customer service."*
Herve Humler, President of The Ritz-Carlton Hotel Company

GOALS ARE YOUR
MISSION STATEMENT

● ● ● ● ●

**"Only those who dare to fail greatly
can ever achieve greatly."
Robert F. Kennedy, American Politician**

● ● ● ● ●

If we have no direction, then just any road can take you to nowhere. Or as Zig Zigler said, "If you aim at nothing, you will hit it every time." And, "Any goal you can properly set is already halfway reached". Creating and fulfilling goals makes life more enjoyable. Without goals, time will escape from you and you will find yourself going aimlessly through each day without direction. You certainly do not have to have goals or follow the ones your employer gives you, but life will be much sweeter if you chase goals with a well-defined end purpose. Knowing who you are, knowing what matters, knowing what you want and knowing what you don't want will help you set and see your goals clearly. If you already have a goal in mind, stating it can be very motivating to pursue and achieve. Once you have completed writing your goals, both long and short term, you have to activate the ones you want to work on, there is no other way to complete them. Why not pick a direction or destination for your life and your career and put your vision, focus, effort and energy equally into achieving all that you can? A dream or idea written down with a completion date will become a goal. A goal broken down into steps will become a plan. A plan put into action will become reality. Decisions when acted upon produce behavior.

IMPACT PLAN:

Specific: Clearly define how, what, when, where, and why. Combine some goals for faster results.

Measurable: Be flexible to change and chart results, you can't measure what you cannot see.

Achievable: A goal too large will defeat your interest but a goal should stretch your capability, always challenge the edge of the envelope.

Realistic: Is it reasonable, do you have the time and resources to reach the goal? If not, have a plan a goal to acquire those needed resources.

Time Bound: Meaningful deadlines for completion create a sense of urgency, without which goals are meaningless.

Focus: Continuously review your goals to assure that you are working on the right ones. Success is often the results of attention to the smallest detail.

Responsibilities: What is on your to do list today and is it relevant to your goals for success. You don't get rich off your day job; you get rich by doing your homework. Self-improvement projects such as to stop or change a bad habit, being healthier or improving relationships are not goals, they are values. You can and should work on those things in the same manner as your Impact Statement, but they are different from goals.

HOW DO I SET GOALS?

Goal setting is something that we hear about throughout our business and personal lives. Very few people actually sit down and articulate the things they want to achieve. A goal is an act of the mind to identify something you want and that you are willing to hold to a course of action to achieve. So, what if you start with some realistic goals for living and working better? First, we brainstorm, write down whatever comes to mind no matter what it is. Don't worry about the format or assigning weight to individual items at this point, just go with whatever comes to you. Everything is important and nothing is too large or small to formulate a vision.

The next step is to take what you've written and make sure it is realistic, achievable and about you. If some items aren't, discard them or rewrite them in a way that they are about you. Now take what you have written and make sure it is worded in a positive way. Meaning that each item is something you want and is worth striving toward. Some parts of your statement must be broken into steps of achievement. Think about how you can make your statement as specific as possible using detailed language. This is the most difficult part of goal setting because it requires deep thought and planning.

ACTION PLAN: Take your goal statement and create a detailed action plan for each statement. Basically, you are answering the questions that arose as you brained stormed and wrote your own wants and needs. Answering these questions should give you more information about what you have already accomplished toward this goal and what the next steps should be. How will you measure progress toward your goals? If you need to create a spreadsheet, start a journal, or find some other method to track your progress then do it. Once again, be as specific as possible.

What are the time frames for you to achieve your goals? Some goals need to happen quickly or at least be within reach but no more than ninety days out because you are learning how work your goals. For larger goals you will need to project into years while developing a variety of project goals to meet along the way. You will need to go back through these steps to evaluate, change and mark off those you have completed. If there are Impact Statements that are too far out of reach at this time you will need to develop, learn, and prepare yourself to attack those goals. Now it is time to activate, why not, you're in sales, you don't have anything else to do.

FOLLOW UP: Now that you have a specific Impact Statement for your goals and an action plan in progress you absolutely must, this part is very important to you, follow-up to evaluate your progress daily, weekly, monthly and annually. Don't be disheartened if there isn't much movement in the short term, it is the journey to the goals that will hold your interest.

ATTITUDE FOR SUCCESS: Demanding goals give you permission to go after the big dreams that require you to grow in order to achieve them. Along the way there will be disappointments and challenges to test your stamina, courage, integrity and perseverance because success follows a series of small events and achievements. Never be afraid to start, the outcome is uncertain but waiting allows opportunities to slip away. Never focus on what isn't working, find a mentor, adapt and overcome, make a change and move on. Never hang out with negative people, the law of attraction states you will become what surrounds you. Never judge your progress by the success of others, their plan is working and yours will to because you are stronger than you think.

It is common but not an error to underestimate how long a goal will take, especially a profound one. Patience is not only a virtue; it is an absolute necessity if you are determined to reach the success you owe yourself. Work on your Impact Plan or some part of your goals every day and eventually you will make them come true.

Success requires hard work and self-discipline, which means you must lean into it and lean into it consistently. Self-discipline is the best avenue to gain self-confidence and success. Always look for opportunities, resources and people who can help you at just the right time. Ask for help and do things to benefit others. Always explore the unknown, trust that the answers and resources you need will appear. Just do it, it will be fun and profitable.

**"Once you have a clear picture of
your priorities that is values,
goals and high leverage activities, organize around them."
Stephen Covey**

**"Begin with the end in mind."
Stephen Covey**

MOTIVATION

• • • • •

"Destiny is no matter of chance. It is a matter of choice.
It is not a thing to be waited for; it is a thing to be achieved."
William Jennings Bryan, American Lawyer

• • • • •

We can all appreciate that people need motivation, but we cannot depend upon others to supply that energy for us. Words are for naught without action and so there are no speakers or recordings or prizes that will supply motivation in the quantity needed to guarantee long-term success. Many will have that fire in the belly when they leave the motivational meeting but unless you know your Craft the flames are doused when you hear the word no and don't know what to do next. This is not an indictment of the presentations by the motivational speakers or the variety of their products, we can learn from each presenter. Most are well worth the money if you know how to apply the philosophy of the speaker, and that is where the devil eats our cake.

When I first began working in sales, I was fortunate to work for a Region Manager who was a great sales manager and whose energy was contagious. His personality made everyone feel special and positive. He was the rarest of our species, he was a natural salesman, but all of the rest of us must be trained and supported. We would have sales meetings, with real food, followed by a sales blitz that required sales revenue at the end of the day. When we left the meeting in teams of two, we would have charged solid walls, breakdown any barrier to make a sale, we were motivated. Unfortunately, most of the salespeople, including me, did not know what to do when the first prospect of the day said no. So, we would negotiate price, never mentioning the value we offered, possibly losing all commission on this sale and or having the sale turned down by management, perhaps getting a reprimand. That scenario is disheartening, and it is also a great de-motivator and a very poor option against knowing your Craft. Many managers use motivation if they can motivate, as a crutch because they do not have the will, knowledge or talent to be successful sales trainers. A manager who cannot lead or motivate may try to drive sales revenue with threats and by imposing their self-will upon the sales staff, but failure soon follows.

Generally, the only people making money from motivational seminars and materials are the ones selling the products but that does not take away from their usefulness or effectiveness. We hear and we see the speaker and the material but absorbing the action words into our focus and process is another matter. The words of successful people are important encouragement for those who need mentoring, and everyone needs a daily dose. Motivational speakers, their books, videos and materials are a valuable part of our training and development, the content should be used to create a superior state of mind and a superior attitude towards your goals and life in general and of equal importance to develop Craftsmanship sales skills. Motivation is only productive if it includes the wisdom to succeed and not merely the increase of emotional stimulation. Frankly speaking, if you cannot find inside yourself the self-esteem and self-inflicted motivation to perform the necessary task a sales position requires, you should get a factory job. However, if you believe in yourself and have pride and dedication and will never quit, you will be successful, and you will like the rewards. There are no books, tapes, DVDs or speakers who can motivate people if they are not self-activated to perform the necessary task to be a successful at length in sales. You must never doubt yourself because doubt kills motivation. Find a quiet place and decide what is important to you and write it down. Buy a digital recorder and state everything you have written and then listen to yourself. How convincing was your argument for a better more successful you? This part is very important to you; talk doesn't get things done only action can do that.

"The secret to getting ahead is getting started."
Mark Twain

MEETINGS & PUBLIC SPEAKING

● ● ● ● ●

"There is only one excuse for a speaker asking
the attention of his audience:
he must have either truth or entertainment for them."
Dale Carnegie, American writer

● ● ● ● ●

BUSINESS MEETINGS: In the traditional sense formal meetings are a waste of time and conference calls are even worse. Weekly staff meetings frequently have more to do with turf or group therapy sessions than with increased efficiency, productivity or profit. Region and/or Division meetings are usually extended crisis management affairs of the most boring and repetitive type leaving the attendees with hours of driving during the worst traffic conditions with little if anything to justify the expense and loss of productivity the meeting caused. The word meeting is cringe worthy in most instances. At the same time, meetings are absolutely necessary, so how can we make meetings productive enough to improve operations and make money?

The Answer: You must always know exactly why you are calling a meeting and what the end results will be.

The people attending have schedules and they should be taken into consideration when possible. Having someone come in while on vacation is a morale killer for everyone. Scheduled meetings should have a prepared agenda with clarity and time frames you can stick to. Advise attendees of the agenda subjects to be discussed in advance in order for them to be prepared and to research. Participants must be engaged in the discussion and not simply be lectured. A lecture is not a business meeting. Remind participants to bring pen and pad to take notes unless they have perfect recall, and that is about as rare as hen's teeth. Staff meetings should be about personnel, procedure, the numbers, problems or customer service and expected results. Have each department report productivity or numbers, personnel situation, plans for correction and how. Be crystal clear in explaining exactly what is to be done and the standard of performance expected and by what date. Allow only the electronics needed for attendees to participate. Assign someone to take and read meeting minutes, your meeting will be worthless if no one remembers what was said or decided in the previous meeting. Start and end your meetings on time.

PUBLIC SPEAKING: Public speaking is different from having a captive audience who are required to pay attention to you in order to stay employed. We worked for a well-respected VP who was a good leader and a fair man, but he started every meeting with, "The reason dinosaurs became extinct is because they failed to adapt or migrate." Good information for a paleontology class but it became a joke in the company although it was no joke in that crisis management atmosphere. For all of his positive traits he missed the opportunity to start his speech with a positive rather than negative connection for his audience.

Prime time comedians, pandering politicians, TV preacher and motivational speakers all connect quickly with their audience because they relate to the self-interests of their audience, coincidentally they all want you to send them your money. So, what motivates people to give you their attention? If it isn't good looks or a sterling personality or a captivating voice you had better have a well-practiced and listen worthy presentation. When I was leading seminars, I wanted to make friends, I made a point to greet everyone as they entered the room with a firm handshake and an invitation to visit the table of snacks and beverages.

At the onset of the meeting I again introduced myself, welcomed them to my seminar and gave an overview of the next hour, pretty standard stuff. I wanted to connect with the entire audience so at certain points I would say, "this part is very important to you." What that statement did was to cause a laser focus on my overhead and on my words, exactly what I wanted to happen. Then I worked that statement into my in-home presentations, I was always at the top of the leader board. The beautiful part is that I rarely got common misunderstandings, stalls or objections. I sold perceived value and made it easy to understand.

How you close is equally important to the body of your message because now it is time for the audience to buy. I had placed a pen and note pad along with a sales agreement at each place setting, so I closed by instructing my audience to completely fill out the contract and sign it. Typically, at the end of my seminars I would take between ten to fifteen signed sales contracts to the office. Converted to income those contracts worked out to around $3000 per hour, not too shabby for a country boy.

Here are a few helpful ideas for holding successful meetings and speaking to the public:

Less is more.

Connect to the audience on a personal level.

Connect with self-interest emotion.

Never scan your audience, it gives the allusion that you are shifty or looking for a weak victim.

Likewise, never look directly into the camera unless you are preaching hells fire.

Be sure your audience can hear you, speak up.

Maintain order and discipline, "this part is very important to you."

Be a time-efficient communicator, start and end on time.

Compliment your audience and thank them for coming.

A little entertainment never hurts, good stories are helpful.

Tell the audience exactly what features and benefits they will gain.

Always end a speech with a call to action, tell them what to do.

It is your stage and you are the star, make the most of it.

"There are certain things in which mediocrity is not to be endured,
such as poetry, music and public speaking."
Jean de la Bruyere. 17ᵗʰ Century **French philosopher**

MENTORS

● ● ● ● ●

"If you light a lamp for someone it will also brighten your own path."
Buddhist Proverb

● ● ● ● ●

There have been people in each of our lives that we well remember, a teacher, someone who reached out when you were down. Or a supervisor who taught you something worthwhile, and those who have made you feel special and loved you. A parent or grandparent, an educator or perhaps a coach who offered advice or that extra bit of instruction or support to help you. Often the ones who make the most difference in our lives are not the ones with the most power or credentials, the most money, or the most awards. But the ones who cared and were sincere about helping you grow into your potential.

The most successful people in life also mentor others. Mentors tend to show up when they are needed the most to lend a hand. They understand the importance of sincere praise and the power of a tutor to help others in the attainment of their dreams. By freely giving their knowledge and experience to others they also reinforce the very basics that have made them successful. We all have traits to assist us in our drive to be successful, and there are many good tools available to help us, but mentoring others is certainly one of our best tools. The results will be to attract others into your sphere of positive influence.

Mentor: Mentors must be experienced professionals who possess a giving attitude and who will embrace the opportunity to help other sellers achieve their individual goals. Mentors can also help to overcome the short comings of company sponsored training. They act as effective role models, demonstrating appropriate behaviors for different situations. Mentors must also have the skills and style the Mentee will want to emulate. For the Craftsman who wants to be the best in their business, to continue to grow their business, to maximize their capabilities, teaching is a gateway to learn and grow. When you Mentor, give your all to everyone you meet because doing the right thing with a little humility will always shine through.

MENTEE: The best knowledge is someone else's experience so if you can learn from what someone else has done, it just makes everything easier. One consistent theme in career and life is persistence. When there is a problem our experience tells us that we should sit down and work out a solution. But some people don't know how to formulate plans to overcome a problem, a Mentor is valuable asset at this point. This part is very important to you, there is always a solution.

If you are a young seller and in need of a help, choose a Mentor who is a sales leader. Be sure to have your Goals Statement finished or in good progress. Look for someone who understands individual career goals and is effective in giving direction and providing motivation that will help a seller achieve the results they want in their careers. Welcome constructive criticism because you are asking for a transfer of ideas and experience you that do not have. A good Mentor will try to give their best advice based on an understanding of your goals and operational knowledge. Discuss your situation in a way that creates further discussion.

Be clear with questions and thoughts, you are using the Mentor's valuable time so be sure he or she understands your wants and needs. Be honest with your mentor, if you need help ask, then be respectfully open minded to the response, if you already know everything you do not need a Mentor.

While mentors should serve as sounding boards, it's important that they be involved in a meaningful two-way dialogue. The mentor needs to be sufficiently flexible but not everyone can change or tailor an approach that makes the seller comfortable. Mentoring should be an opportunity for the Mentor to learn, too. Be open to joint field activity, joint fieldwork is the heart of mentoring. It's in real life sales situations where you discover how their sales approach and presentations are working. The Mentor needs the ability to understand and explain products and selling techniques in such a way that the Mentee will become a person with whom the public will want to do business. Building the Mentee's skills enable him to ask the right questions and to think tactically and strategically. The tactical is at the point of sale, and the strategic is the overall direction for reaching your goals.

"My mentor said, 'Let's go do it,' not 'You go do it.'
How powerful when someone says, 'Let's!"
Jim Rohn, American Entrepreneur, Author and Motivational Speaker

SALES

To become a sales Craftsman, you must acquire skill and knowledge.

NEGOTIATING FOR SUCCESS

● ● ● ● ●

"In business as in life, you don't get what you deserve
you get what you negotiate."
Dr, Chester L. Karrass, author of Effective Negotiating

● ● ● ● ●

What is a negotiation? A negotiation is a discussion aimed at reaching an agreement, an action or to process a transfer of ownership. Each negotiation is embedded in the larger context of co-beings that involve empathy and awareness of a common goal or condition. A negotiation is a strategic conflict and much like in an athletic contest momentum is of great importance.

This chapter is about arriving at a point where a sale can be made by finding solutions to a stopping point. A sale may be setting a difficult appointment or the signing of a contract, but each is a negotiation. You will negotiate solutions to seek a mutually beneficial win - win relationship with prospects because you want repeat business, to continue revenue capture and to meet profit goals. A Craftsman never negotiates over problems, the Craftsman negotiates over a better solution.

The art of negotiating is an essential skill of the modern sales Craftsman. Every person in our lives is a negotiation because relationships are in a constant state of negotiation and balance. What you say and how you say it in the opening moments are the prospect's perception and will set the climate for the negotiation. How to negotiate isn't always easy to learn, it is a skill that has to be developed rather than inherited. It should go without saying, leave personalities out of your thoughts and don't take anything personally so that you may see your opportunities more objectively.

A problem is not a no answer or a stopping point, but it does give you a direction to negotiate to a deal closed. One tactic to resolve a problem is to ask the prospect to offer a solution then lead the now buyer to the desired results. While the prospect is talking you are connecting, learning and building on the relationship. The prospect will quickly know whether you are working for a win-win solution, or if you are a shark circling blood in the water.

**The most typical buyer attitudes towards
a seller, product or service are
objection, indifference, skepticism, and acceptance.**

Objection is because the prospect is in opposition to you, the product or the investment.

Indifference is because there is no interest, or the benefit is insufficient to satisfy wants and needs.

Skepticism is because the prospect is doubtful you or your product can produce the desired value.

Acceptance is because the prospect has a positive view of you, your product and the expected value.

The Negotiation Process:

Empathy: The seller, in order to negotiate effectively, must empathize with the prospects point of view or belief and work alongside the prospect to find a solution. To approach an issue from the prospects view and discuss each other's perceptions is a good way to start negotiations. There are two competing sides working to a center point, therefore there are two truths.

Saving Face: The win – win solutions, for both seller and prospect, require a compromise where all parties are satisfied with the deal. This approach is less arbitrary, and thus, it is a more acceptable form of the prospects perspective and it builds a more lasting relationship. A meaningful negotiated solution requires communication that equalizes the prospects position in order to not lose face. In short do not insult or embarrass the prospect.

Attentive Listening: Listening and hearing are not the same thing. Attentive listening involves paying close attention to what is being said verbally and nonverbally. Ask direct questions for definition and clarification from the prospect because the negotiation is special and all about the prospect.

Communication: Negotiating is about maneuvering and it is always about the prospect's wants and needs. Before stating a point, determine exactly what and how you wish to communicate and state the point clearly to gain agreement with the prospect. Summarize the points of mutual agreement with some detail being careful of information overload. Beware of cultural norms especially if you are outside your comfort territory.

Negotiation Styles: **Competing – The Bully**   **Win – Lose**
                              Avoiding – The Politician   **Lose – Lose**
                              Accommodating – The Doormat **Lose – Win**
                              Collaborating - The Negotiator   **Win – Win**

**Collaborating a win – win solution is the
only acceptable method for a
Sales Craftsman.**

Unless the prospects attitude is acceptance, signs your contract and hands over a referral, the seller must negotiate a change in the prospects position. The seller must find solutions for the other attitudes and be comfortable with "what's in it for me" being the prospects solution. Trial closing questions are to acquire a buying opinion or conviction, close questions are to acquire a buying decision. Negotiate only after giving your complete presentation and the investment is on the table, no is the opening of your negotiating position. Never put money on the table before a clear interest is given in the product.

Listen to what is said in opposition and what is expressed in the prospects body language to identify the key problem, then define the main points as presented to you. Ask open ended questions but be prepared for tactical and body language responses, do not react but be comfortable and ask more questions. Speak deliberately but slowly being sure to pronounce your words clearly, nodding and smiling. Information is your greatest strength during a negotiation and conversation is of tremendous help because good conversation is the cornerstone of productive negotiations. Don't fear your own silence in the negotiating process but have patience, it is the companion of wisdom and will work for you to a solution. You want the prospect to speak more than you because you are the solution.

Objections are statement or actions by the prospect that indicate resistance or an unwillingness to buy but are also useful tactics to get a lower priced offer. The price only prospect will manufacture a problem over money, but price only is a lose - lose deal for both sides. It's important to understand that all prospects act in their own best interest and are motivated to negotiate from that position, as are you. They do not necessarily need to meet the needs of someone else in order to reach a workable agreement. When you face the reluctant buyer, desperation is your expected reaction. Desperation has a stench about it that empowers the prospect to seek further reductions in price. Sales Craftsmen are never desperate to close because they have strategy, knowledge and skill.

Listen to how statements are made in connection with what was said by the prospect, they may conflict. A few, serious buyer or not, will enjoy the game even if they don't understand it and try to intimidate the seller with irritating behavior. Make sure that you strip out all of your emotion and deal with the facts, trust your training and sell them something.

References:

The Psychology of Selling – Brian Tracy
Secrets of Power Negotiating – Roger Dawson
Getting to Yes – Roger Fisher & William Ury

PROSPECTING

● ● ● ● ●

"Our greatest weakness lies in giving up.
The most certain way to succeed is
always to try just one more time." Thomas Edison, American Inventor

● ● ● ● ●

PROSPECTING: Prospecting from the sales trainer's podium sounds like the hills are dripping with jewels and laden in gold bullion. What the untrained seller hears is load all of your stuff on a donkey and go walk in the desert until you die. Negative outlooks will inevitability result in negative outcomes, prospecting is about optimism and selling you. What is a prospect? A prospect is a person or group of people who are potential customers, everyone else is merely a suspect. There is a path, however rocky at first, to achieve financial success by seeking to find new prospects and customers through prospecting. There will be temporary defeats but that is not failure, failure is to quit trying.

A longtime friend owns a Pre-owned Auto Dealership where he spreads a few pennies in walkways around his inventory. People pick up a penny and say, "this my lucky day," my friend thinks, "yes, it is." I asked about the pennies and his answer was, "feed the lot and the lot feeds you." This is an excellent definition of prospecting, feed your sales funnel and the sales funnel will feed you.

The list of prospecting targets is endless, but someone has to make a contact with someone else, make a connection and engage the prospect and form a relationship. There are people so adept at prospecting that they do not accept marketing leads of any form and that was before electronic media was developed to assist. There are too many to name but here is a short list, my favorites are Seminars and EXPOs because I want person to person exposure to as many people as possible.

Current Customers - Referrals - Past Customers - Orphaned Customers (*originating seller retired*) -

Lost Leads - Pending Leads - Seminar Leads – Direct Mail – Telemarketing – Business List - Friends

Family - Cold Calls – Face to Face Calls – LinkedIn – Facebook or another online venue

QUALIFYING THE PROSPECT: Qualified sales prospects and leads will have a higher return on your investment of time and higher closing ratio; therefore, we must separate the prospect from the suspect. To qualify a prospect, you must determine whether or not they have an awareness of need, a since of urgency to buy, a willingness to listen, have the authority to buy and have the financial resources to make the purchase. If the answers are yes, they become worthy of your time and energy. Take the natural momentum of the prospect and draw it to you.

Ask the prospect if there is a problem, then isolate the problem. Build on to the problem by finding the effect or impact of the problem? Relieve the pressure with an offer to present a solution, now you are negotiating. Secure the appointment, offer a solution, it is as simple as that.

COLD CALLS & CALL RELUCTANCE: My first encounter with cold calling and the resulting call reluctance is common among sellers who must depend upon training to supply at least the minimum of knowledge and encouragement to achieve success in sales. I had spent a few weeks learning the product through the eyes of the service department and then an uneventful day with each of the three sellers on staff, no one sold anything. On the fourth day the manager threw a telephone directory more at me than to me and ordered me to find prospects and make a sale on that day. I had no script to guide me and not the slightest suggestion of how to make a cold call and in fact it was my first attempt. Yep, the very first person who answered called me terrible names and insulted my heritage, starting several generations back, then suggested I do a few impossible functions with the phone. Totally confused, and a little angry, I did exactly what the other three sellers were doing, I joined them at Ma's Café for breakfast. Most people are nice to callers and some are a little more firm in response but only a few people who answer are truly ugly to the caller. Those people must have very sad lives and are probably rude to nearly everyone whether by phone in person and it is a serious mistake to give their outburst any credibility. Also, there are many types of scams today, which may fuel a hostile response, and not just online, they knock on our doors and call us on our phones. Why would anyone trust someone they don't know and who intrudes on their privacy by cold calling them? With these and other negatives in mind why do managers promote cold calling when it is so difficult to do and when some, perhaps most, sellers believe it is a complete waste of time, plus no one wants to do it? The answer is because advertising leads are too expensive and erratic to rely upon as a constant source of prospects and revenue capture.

Cold calling although it is not the Golden Goose of leads most certainly can lead to gold in your nest when done consistently and with flavor. It may well be your last resort and you may not like to do it because you don't have enough information about the person you are calling, but if you have no prospects to present to you have nothing to lose. The mental pain of cold calling is still better than the pain of having bills and no money. When used professionally cold calling has both a valid and productive place in the sales process, especially for the new or inexperienced seller who has little if any training and zero in the sales funnel. No matter what your industry happens to be your existing customers are the Gold Mine of leads that you can up sell and ask for referrals if you and your company has in fact validated value to the customer.

Some salespeople have superstitions built in as to when they should make cold calls on certain days, and time of day, some may even have a lucky shirt. The truth of the matter is that no one knows the best time to call. How could you? Your call might be just what the prospect needs on that day and at that time. There is no way you can know their minds, and it's a waste of time to try. The odds of success are improved more by the content of your call than by the time of day you choose to make it. Making calls now is better than making calls later because if you are not a right now person you are not going to be successful in sales. We sellers are creatures of habit too, so it stands to reason if you have a habit of fear or anxiety about making a simple phone call, failure is in your future. You can choose to have great habits through goal setting and then attacking in fractions or in leaps, it is up to you to be assertive with yourself. Cold calling is challenging, and it requires significant amount of mental energy to focus and discipline yourself to make the calls at the beginning, but it will become a good habit. You will need mental toughness but the sooner you defeat the fear the sooner you can start making money. Business author B.J. Gallagher coined the phrase *"yes lives in the land of no."*

Now that we have established cold calling is necessary, we need to understand where and how to start making connections that will lead to relationships that lead to presentations and to sales. If you have read this far you know how strongly I support the use of digital voice and video recordings to practice presentations and yes cold calls are a presentation to sell an appointment. Using readily available technology and fine-tuning as you go you can develop the skills necessary to become an expert. Within a very short time depending upon your willingness to grow yourself, and to your advantage you will not sound like the dreaded tele-marketer. You must work on the tone of your voice as well as the content of your message, make yourself sound friendly in a business-like manner. You will know it is right when you listen to yourself sell an appointment to yourself.

You will need a script to guide you until your proficiency improves to the point you no longer need it. Your script must be sincere, about the prospect and have an opening to capture the prospects attention and then a statement or question to steer the response. It must include using the prospects name and should include asking if he/she has time to talk. You will also need a professional and comfortable way to exit the call with an appointment. If you don't have a script write it yourself, it is simple to do but keep the length well under a minute, 20 to 30 seconds is ideal. Speak slower during your cold call after all you have twenty seconds to connect and engage. Stop here and hold your breath for twenty seconds, see, it's a long time. The Craftsman will operate at a slower pace but is more effective knowing that there is no need to launch into sales presentation of products and services when selling an appointment. They understand that their marketing messages and conversations are crucial to their success and therefore must be well directed and point on delivered. Your first call is to make a connection with the intent of building a relationship with the prospect and then an appointment.

The initial cold call can be used as a warmup conversation to establish common ground, mutual respect leading to an appointment with the prospect. In this call bring attention to the prospects wants and needs, the seller and the sellers value proposition and/or product. You can email or connect on LinkedIn or friend on Facebook, or make another call? You must always be moving towards a relationship to the point where you can meet over coffee or an appointment for presentation. Once you have established a rapport you can start to engage but listen carefully and look for referral opportunities. Now you are taking control.

Using the shotgun system of calling is a form of self-torture, easier to use a hammer on your head. But the Cross-Reference Directory, Thomas Directory of Business or even the telephone directory, if used by Zip Code, can help you build a targeted list to approach. The more targeted your list, the greater your odds of connecting with interested prospects. If your prospect is Federal, Industrial or Business Research, learn and understand the issues or concerns they face and who makes the decisions before calling or visiting. Knowing about the prospects business and having the right crafted questions to ask and with the right message for the situation gives you credibility and open the door for a relationship. Even if you fail to gain an appointment, you have begun developing a relationship, and you have begun to establish your strong desire to work with the prospect and make a difference in their lives or business.

Choose your words phrases carefully because words matter. Don't waste the prospects time and your energy asking, "how are you today." It is irrelevant unless the prospect leads into health or personal issues, then it is a lost call. Simply confirm that you are speaking to the prospect then deliver your introduction. Do not launch into your presentation on the call as it is easy to say NO over the phone and you are only selling an appointment.

Everyone loves to hear their name; be sure you do not mispronounce no matter how many times you have to practice saying that name aloud. To mispronounce a prospects name without an apology and without an effort to get it right is a lost call.

Practice your introduction, need I say it, with digital technology until you sound natural and comfortable and do it until you can't get it wrong. Learn your script and make it interesting. You have a much better chance of making an appointment if you avoid being like everyone else. If the seller comes on as timid, too strong, too cheerful, too upbeat it is a lost call, it is the well-rehearsed seller with a message that wins.

Have the right questions for top executives and be careful not to insult.

Free estimate with no obligation is tired and over used language even if it is true.

"Actually, the reason I'm calling, "means I want your money.

Unconditional guarantee means there will be conditions.

"If I could show you a way," means I want to take a substanual amount of your time and money.

"Nobody can sell this cheaper," means the seller can't sell it cheaper.

"I'll be honest with you," means the caller is not being honest.

It is not complicated, and cold calling is much better than being poor. It is only a phone call, it's not a big deal. The world will not end if someone says no, but someone will say yes, and you will gain a nice commission. Enjoy the moment and take someone special to dinner and celebrate. Then, do it again.

INTRODUCTION: Sales Craftsman know that they must sell themselves first, therefore the cold call introduction is no less important than your sales presentation. The introduction is in fact a sales presentation. The script you have written must define you, what you offer, your market, and any distinctive benefits you can provide. Refine the script until you can say it effectively in twenty seconds or less, which is about as long as most prospects attention span for cold calls will hold.

EXAMPLE: This example will take about twenty seconds to deliver. Hello is this Mr. Jones, thank you sir. My name is John Smith and I represent Personal Islands Real-estate Development and Construction Company. We do all types of construction including windows, roofing, siding and general construction including concrete work. Bill Adams gave me your name and number saying perhaps I could help with an ongoing project you have; do you have a few minutes to talk? If the answer is yes, continue to sell the appointment, if it is no then ask would like me to call at a better time for you. Sell yourself to get the appointment but remember the call is about the prospect.

GETTING PROSPECTS TO RETURN CALLS: As often as not your call will go to the prospects voice mail and your job is to give them a reason to want to return your call. If you are calling a referred prospect or one from a mutual connection state who the referral came from by name and how you are connected. We are all hammered with robot calls and the last thing your prospect wants to hear is a lengthy message. Have a specific reason to make the call and stick to that reasoning. You know your reason for the call but what is the benefit for the prospect? Involve or partner with the prospect in the initial call stating the benefits for the prospect. No gain for the prospect, no return call for you. Phone tag is a sure way to lose the prospects attention and the appointment so be sure to tell prospects the best times to reach you then be available. Give your prospects the opportunity to reach you in other ways. Show your commitment to connecting with the prospect by offering other means of contact such as texting or any electronic method. When a prospect calls you back let them lead the conversation but be prepared for a short call. Give the prospect a reason to meet you by appointment.

THE GATEKEEPER: The Gatekeeper is rarely if ever the buying power, but the buying power gives the Gatekeeper's judgement and advice credibility. They are in place to protect the prospect from you, and most of them enjoy the power that comes with the title. They come in a variety of fashions from an administrative person who reads every email and letter while controlling the delete button. Or perhaps it could be a junior management person and sometimes even a wife or relative. It doesn't matter who the gatekeeper is or their attitude towards you, they are busy, and they have authority over you. They are people too so be kind to them, engage them and try to make a personal connection and sell the gatekeeper on selling your appointment, because until you do you are not a trusted resource.

If no one is aware of your impending visit, it is cold call. Some sellers go on about warm calls, they are lacking in professional behavior having been convinced that they can assert themselves into an appointment. An assertive poster with the Gatekeeper may work if you have the presence of 007 and the voice of an angel, otherwise take a seat on the end. The management who teach warm calls are attempting to soften your mental picture and are only interested in numbers, they do not have your best interest in mind.

My admin staff always advised me of who was rude to or assertive with them and I would never do business with someone who was rude to my people. The Gatekeeper can be your best friend, develop a relationship. If you have a referral it may be easier to get access, but it is still best to call and advise the gatekeeper you will be visiting and state the time, or you may not have an appointment.

REFERENCE:

How to Win Friends and Influence People by Dale Carnegie
Overcoming Call Reluctance by Ken Dooly

TRADE SHOWS: The purpose for a trade show event is to draw attention to your products and services, your purpose is to connect with people and then engage them in conversation. Most cities today have various Fairs, Mall Expos, and large events. Buy a booth or two and display your services and products in an appealing manner. Purchase a nice mid-range propane grill or some other appliance that is appropriate and a professional sign that states REGISTER TO WIN ME. Dollar or percentage discounts will lead to current customers expecting something for free. A must have is a professional looking ballot box that stands tabletop height from the floor or just a little more, put your Logo on it facing the traffic. A cardboard box does not inspire confidence and a volume of ballots in the grill is the opposite of an expectation to win.

Working a seminar or trade show is tough on the feet but when managed with enthusiasm there will be an abundance of leads. Schedule shifts of not more than four hours rotating people in and out. Everyone who expects to share in the leads must work shifts including all levels of local management. Have a comfortable pair of shoes because there will be no chairs or stools, we are there to work and not sit. Customers get a negative impression of salespeople sitting and it is probably an accurate assessment.

Have an abundance of material to hand out even if it is obsolete, it will be in the trash tomorrow anyway. What we want is a name and phone number on a ballot and in the box. Engage everyone passing if it is no more than, (did you register to win your grill.) The questions about your products and services will come automatically if you follow these simple rules.

I have a few proud moments from these shows, once there was an Insurance Agent a table or two away who stated quite angrily that we were too aggressive, and he would never be close us again. While that seller sat in a comfortable chair and waited, I took three thousand leads from that show and routinely collected more than ten thousand EXPO leads annually using this process, they were dispersed between eight to ten sellers. Of course, each lead must be recorded and follow-up on for disposition.

SALES CONTEST: I have never designed a sales contest for my sellers, but I used the above systems to the maximum. We were always in blitz mode so when the Corporate or the Region Manager had money to give away, we were happy to take it. We were winners and liked to win and we liked the recognition we received form winning. However, if sales contest are your route be sure the prize is worth the effort because trinkets and small change won't get more than a sand bagged sale or two. I was in a meeting with other senior RMs discussing how to increase sales through spirit and morale, when the chatter took a break one of the older men said in his gravelly voice, "the only thing that improves sales is selling." The wisdom of that statement is that *success breeds success.*

A wonderful method we used was a 3 X 3-inch form for the Pest Control Route Managers to ask their customers to sign granting permission for one of our sellers to visit and inspect the property for termites. The PCRM received $50 for each closed sale. This was a good November project for everyone to have Christmas money. Review service contracts or insurance policies etc. to find prospects in your existing customer base who may want to spend some money.

One other method we used was residential survey around new accounts that was very effective. It started as one of those magic wands Middle Management gets excited about but had little substance. The excitement was a sheet of paper with two questions on it. My team brainstormed and then field tested an actual survey. We had fifteen questions that defined ownership, type of construction, age of structure length of residence, what the owner believed was the most common type of pest, and any known treatment to the home. At the end of the survey, we made an appointment for a future date. We never entered the house until the appointment date. A survey isn't worth much if it doesn't result in a qualified prospect and an appointment.

REFERRALS: Referrals come to us through those we have served well but in greater abundance from those with whom we have built a firm and lasting relationship. What is the quickest way to build rapport and encourage a relationship with people? Just smile, and it really is that simple. Smiles are contagious, even with your Mother in Law. Get that ole girl to smiling and you are home free. Smiles create a positive presence and response from other people. A smile says that we are friends and that we are happy and safe to be with. A smile encourages people to lower their guard and be receptive to you. Having a sense of humor can help create and build on relationships because people want to be around happiness and laughter, everyone wants to feel good. Humor is a great icebreaker that can make a problem manageable, but it has to be humorous to the prospect. Being a great listener invites others to share and opens doors you didn't know were there. Listening offers the opportunity to share your life experiences and hopes and dreams. Listening well builds trust in you and makes a statement that conveys confidence in you without you saying one word and is a strong relationship builder. I was in high school and had a lump in my throat when the prettiest girl in school smiled and said, "you are such a good listener." I didn't speak for two years after that. When a customer offers you a referral, he is accepting a vested interest in what happens and what you do because it reflects upon him or her. You are now doubly accountable to give the new prospect your best efforts and a stellar value presentation if you want to keep that recommendation door open.

Are you recommendation worthy, how often do you follow-up with your customers or do you ever? How will you know if they are happy enough with the deal to compliment you with a recommendation if you don't ask? How firm is your relationship with your customers, and do they consider doing business with you a value proposition? There is no way to know unless you ask, you may get the referral, but you may also get the boot in which case you have some work to do. It is not enough to give value if the customer doesn't recognize they have acquired something unique and special, you have to tell them and show them. Doing a value call but still better a face-to-face meeting is a very good method of collecting referrals.

The next best way in my view is at closing when you are busy filling out your contract and the customer is happy but has empty hands, push a legal pad and pen over and say, "if you know anyone I may be of service to please give me a name and number." Several reasons for this method, the know, like and trust factor is in place, everyone is happy, you have earned permission to ask for a recommendation and the customer will not reopen any objection or stall conversation while searching for your next presentation, keep the customer's hands and thoughts busy helping you. We used this method and always had a prospect to present to.

It's not just who you know, it's about who they know so leave a few of your business cards with all of your customer.

WANTS AND NEEDS

● ● ● ● ●

"If you do not ask the right questions, you do not get the right answers. A question asked in the right way often leads to its own answer. Asking questions is the A–B–C of diagnosis. Only the inquiring mind solves problems".
Edward Hodnett, Author of The Art of Problem solving

● ● ● ● ●

Questions tell the prospect you are interested in them and Craftsman care enough about the prospect to ask at least four open-ended questions about wants and needs. What kind of questions? Who, what, when, where, how, why, could, would, should, tell me what else, please describe that for me and tell me about that are the first words in an open-ended question that requires a thoughtful if not an at length answer? Always ask at least four open ended questions. Closed ended questions will get you a one-word answer, we do not ask those questions. After you have asked the right questions to discover evidence, which is also leverage, either seen by you or given by the prospect. Known evidence is a powerful leverage at close.

Why do you need to establish credibility and trust alongside a relationship with the prospect and not just tell our story and ask for the money? Because you can't negotiate with a someone who will not or does not talk to you.

What is the difference between wants and needs? Needs are situational in nature and the cause for a change in present behavior. Wants are the benefits, solutions and results of making a purchase.

Prospects in any purchase situation are focused on solving their wants and needs and the seller must acquire information in order to solve that problem and present a value-oriented solution. Inertia, lack of action, is a formidable foe in the world of sales without a solid relationship with the prospect. But with a few probing questions, you can get your prospect and your sales production moving in the right direction. The most valuable thing you can do after asking is to listen with interest.

An early question must be to establish purchase authority, will council or someone other than the prospect makes the buying decision. Try to get all parties together for your presentation because no one can transfer your work to other ears, those ears will hear that it cost too much.

When you make the purchase of a car, computer, cell phone or even a home there are unknowns and questions before you purchase. Your prospect is in the same position while sitting in front of you. Do you want an eager sales representative throwing his precious 'pitch' at you or a Craftsman addressing your wants and needs as efficiently and effectively as possible? Not surprisingly, the answer to this question is the same for every business, in every industry, and in every culture, and in every gender. Prospects are much more interested in addressing their needs than being "sold" on your solutions. This is where a seemingly small difference in semantics translates into a significant increase in sales effectiveness and productivity. As it turns out, solving a customer's problem and providing a solution are basically the same thing. You can't solve a problem without providing and proving a solution, nor can you provide a value solution without solving a problem.

Still, there is a huge difference between being a "problem solver" and a "solution provider." The difference is perception. Prospects today are more focused on addressing their goals, objectives, wants, needs and desires, than they are willing to be on the receiving end of a sales presentation. So, adapting a problem solver mindset can give the seller a significant advantage over the traditional solution provider mentality in today's increasingly competitive marketplace. While everyone knows that success in selling is about building mutually beneficial relationships, sellers who focus on solving their customer's problems can expect to sell substantially more solutions.

OK, where do we start? Practicing the 'Taking Control' chapter and learning to ask questions then attentive listening are a great place to start. Whether the meeting is in a home or office there must be a period of warm conversation that is of great importance to closing the sale. You are finding areas of life that are of mutual interest and common ground. You can ask questions with open ended answers allowing the prospect to inform you about his interest. It can be about cars, sports, the weather or just about anything that is a bonding element provided you show actual interest. Facts and figures are soon forgotten but stories are told and retold but be sure the prospect is always the hero. It isn't more appointments we need; it is better conversation. How long does the warmup time last, as long as it takes to establish a relationship with friendly confidence in you?

When I first started in sales, we were not allowed to take an order over the phone and we did not under any circumstance present to a woman unless her husband, the purchasing power, was present. Theory was that when he arrived, she would give him the price but not the value of the price and he would reject the proposal out of hand. He would probably instruct her to call another company and why not if it is only about price. Old school thinking was manipulation, intimidation, flattery and control but in this new business environment none of that will be successful for you. Today, as always, women are as prepared as anyone to make financial and business decisions. A female prospect may be less willing to share bonding experiences with a male seller for obvious reasons and that is OK because it is a business meeting not a date. A compliment about surroundings or decor are appropriate but not at length. Otherwise a female prospect should be treated with the same respect and careful evaluation of wants and needs as any other prospect. That includes a professional presentation and an explanation of benefits without jargon.

RULES FOR LISTENING: Start with a warmup period, be attentive because people know when you are interested and paying attention to what they are saying and what is important to them. This time period is not about you and no one cares about you. Ask questions without interrupting the answer because without a good question a good answer has nowhere to go. Now is the time to listen and gain confidence from the prospect during this interactive process. Your posture and body language are telling signs of how involved you are to help them. Nodding, lean in, repeating what the prospect said, taking notes, and an emotional response is acceptable. Check your understanding of everything the prospect says and asking for clarification. Good questions wake people up and get them involved in the process. Short questions will help you probe deeper and if it is emotional by all means show empathy or the appropriate sympathy.

Never ever never, pass judgement or prejudge the prospects ability to buy. Large orders are regularly taken from people who look like they couldn't afford a cup of coffee.

If there is a period of silence repeat the prospects last statement or fill that time with an open-ended question. Craftsman ask better questions and therefore get better answers.

The approach to problem solving is largely on intellectual grounds, routing the prospect from dilemma to decision with words diagrams and illustrations. The stages of progress begin with identifying the problem, stating it and thereby giving it form, analyzing it, and going on to the types of questions it may arouse. Speculation, logic and analogy are all factors in problem solving just as in science, while as an art experience, imagination and intuition will play their part. The method then completes the cycle from recognition to attack to action and will apply in any problem-solving situation.

**Knowledge is having the right answer,
intelligence is asking the right question.**

TAKING CONTROL

• • • • •

Control your own destiny, or someone else will.
Jack Welch, American business executive

• • • • •

Coming from a very conservative professional background, sales, although I believed I could do it well, was new to me and I had many questions. I listened to anyone of experience who spoke hoping to catch some pearl of knowledge and not appear to be as green as I certainly was. I read books written mostly by the self-proclaimed sales experts, the results were both worthwhile and a waste of time. During a training meeting a well-respected and likable Division Sales Manager said that in a sales presentation you must take control, just tell them the story and ask for the money. Sounds simple right? A classmate asked how to take control while visiting someone's home or business. I thought it to be a good question, as I also wanted more definition. The answer that came back in an assertive tone was, "just take control, you know." No, I did not know and neither did my fellow classmates because only a few of the forty people in that class survived to enjoy a career with what was and is a great company. Most salespeople receive enough product knowledge to get by on and are then sent to the field unarmed. However, taking control in the sales process is a very important part of being successful and it must be done, plus the prospect expects you to take control. Later and with some experience I could see the answer to the question of how to take control is really very simple, but it is a process

Everything in life is a process that can be broken down into small steps that can reach great heights. For example, you may be hungry.

First you must decide what and where you want to eat, and then the food has to be prepared, served and consumed. If you are eating in a restaurant you may have to wait to be seated and a gratuity for the server is appropriate, there may be travel involved. You cannot eat, dress, drive, work, buy a lottery ticket, make love or much of anything else without a process of activity. A process of activity is needed to gain an end result. In this case to gain enough confidence from the prospect to form a relationship leading to a sales presentation and a closed sale.

The Law of Attraction states that you will attract into your life whether wanted or unwanted to whatever you give your energy, focus and attention. Since we know we won't make a sale in the first few minutes but that we can easily lose it, we must project a professional image and do it with a smile. People are conditioned to evaluate the seller on sight and people like people who offer a friendly smile to them. So, if I want to make a sale, I must create a professional image, and do it with a smile for the outset of my arrival. We are constantly giving off vibrations of energy, some that are good while others may be bad for us. These vibrations are received by all of those around us. The universe responds to whatever you are offering by giving you more of whatever you are vibrating. It doesn't care whether it is good for you or bad for you; it simply responds to your vibration. The prospect will always know whether or not you are sincere.

The process of taking control is similar for any type of outside sales that will usually take place in the prospects home or business, fortunately for us the prospect expects us to take control. Do not focus on the outcome, focus on the process to acquire the desired outcome. Focus on process not outcome. When you focus on process you can quickly gain trust and establish credibility while building a relationship.

The reason for taking control is to set a stage that is conducive to your success and that is exactly what the prospect needs and expects from you. Now that we control the stage, we bring energy to the transfer of belief and create confidence within the relationship. We then present with great clarity a value package that cannot be refused. Think of taking control as the **"Rules of Ceremony."**

1. First impressions must be professional and setting the mood is vital in any sales presentation and a good mood will make you stand out. Have positive thoughts about the prospect in your mind no matter the condition of your surroundings. Dress professionally and be aware of your appearance at all times, ensure that your breath is fresh, onion, highly spiced or garlicky foods should be avoided prior to the meeting. You are a guest and offending your host will get you a quick exit, but no commission dollars.

2. Do not smoke, not only is it bad for your health but the odor permeates your clothes and is very offensive to those who do not smoke. If you chew tobacco, find a truck-driving job, no one wants to observe the disgusting behavior associated with the spit cup.

3. Take care of your body functions prior to arrival. It rude and offensive behavior to ask for access to their bathroom, particularly if you leave offensive odors.

4. Park out of the way even if you have to walk. If you park in the prospect's driveway blocking ingress and egress someone will ask you to move during your presentation and you will lose the prospects concentration and the sale. It pays to be humble.

5. When you are visiting a residence use what is provided by the prospect to alert the prospect you have arrived. Use the doorbell or door knocker and step well back from the door so that you may be clearly observed and are not threatening to crash the door, if there is no answer use your cell phone to call. Do not assault glass doors or windows with heavy items like a pocketknife or large coin and do not peak in the window unless you are aware of a distress situation, they may think you are a pervert and call the law, it has happened.

6. Eye contact is an essential tool for influencing others. Looking at your prospect when speaking conveys confidence and respect but prolonged eye contact can project hostility and it is rude. Ma'am, Sir, please and thank you are pleasing manners, use them every time without fail.

7. Smile. A smile softens hearts and lights up everyone's eyes because it is an invitation for others to interact with you. No smile no MOJO.

8. As you approach the home or business carefully observe all that is about you, landscaping, vehicles, boat and anything unusual. Once inside you will need conversational items for the warmup in addition to opening the wants and needs dialog that will lead the prospect into your presentation. Intention determines attention. There will be items inside that can lead to conversation as well, do not get involved in controversial subjects but if you can't avoid it agree with your prospect. This is where the sale is made because you are finding common ground with the prospect and people buy from people they like. Virtually everyone has some level of buyer remorse and or resistance during your presentation and one excellent way to relieve that stress is to revisit your common ground. I learned that late one night in a home a hundred miles from my own home. The man was a little league baseball couch: there was plenty of evidence in the home and I had developed my common ground on that subject. Having finished my presentation and ask for the money the wife said, "we'll have to think about it", the dreaded stall. Stalls are often emotional barriers and therefore more difficult to overcome than objections. Thinking I had lost the sale but wanting a clear opening for another opportunity, I sat back in my chair and reopened the conversation about little league baseball. About five minutes had passed when I noticed a change in the tension at the table, my prospects were relaxed, then the husband turned to his wife and said, "I think we should go ahead" and she agreed.

9. Warm down before you leave, and you will have fewer cancellations waiting for you on your return to the office. Sell yourself first and then sell value but always be humble, it works.

10. On the morning after the sale write a thank you note and put it in the mail, and do not forget to ask for a referral. Not all of us have a legible handwriting but most of us can print well enough to get by. This is a simple business communication tactic that can

have a huge impact on how your customers and prospects feel about you and your organization. The handwritten, personal note is effective in building strong customer relationships and is smart-marketing strategy. If you don't make your prospects and customers feel important, they'll find someone else who will. In my offices I would not accept a sales contract unless the thank you note was attached.

11. The ability to control the conversation and ask good questions is a critical skill for salespeople. The right questions at the right time get the best answers and cause the prospect to like and respect you. Empathy, feeling what the prospect feels will aid the seller in learning how to ask the right questions will also allow you to dramatically improve your production. It also moves the sales process forward because you have common ground. This part is very important to you, practice asking questions and conversation with yourself on your digital recorder and/or on video, do it until you can't get it wrong. Showing interest in the prospect will close more business than attempting to get them interested in you.

12. There are those who will scoff at this method of engagement. Their resistance may be a lack of vision because of the simplicity of the plan. It could be that ego, intellect or their maturity prevent them from supporting any system other than "we always did it this way," and so they dismiss the process. High earnings in a sales career is a learned Craft honed to a razor edge by professional people. It works, do it.

READING THE PROSPECT

● ● ● ● ●

"Talk to a man about himself and he will listen for hours."
Benjamin Disraeli, British statesman

● ● ● ● ●

Wouldn't it be wonderful if the prospect asked you if they could please buy your product? It happens all of the time, not just for order takers but for professional Sales Craftsman who understand the social styles and adapt their sales approach accordingly. It is often physical jesters that express interest and a willingness to buy or not. But to know the difference the seller must know how to read the nonverbal communications from the customer.

Nonverbal communication is so important that decision makers in government and business hire body language experts to read the social styles and personalities of the opposition. Prosecution and defense attorneys hire specialist to evaluate juries in an attempt to project a certain and desirable outcome of trials. With these facts in mind you can not afford to not understand nonverbal communication.

Without doubt the most recognizable nonverbal communication between humans is during rush hour traffic when some jerk who deep in his heart of gold believes his time is more valuable than yours and has just cut you off in traffic. As an added perk he is now waving the Hawaiian Good Luck sign in your direction. He may also offer some verbal drivers education advice along with some more good luck. Best response is to smile and wave in a friendly manner after all everyone will arrive at the next red light at precisely the same time and a friendly jester will steal his thunder, deal closed you win. You read his body language and understand that this driver has issues that scream his life is full of anger and frustration. Now that you have an understanding of this driver you know how to handle the situation to your best interest.

Reading the prospect is one of the most interesting parts of the sales process, it is great fun and elevates the seller professionally when they understand it. Before you can even hope to make a sale, you must first capture your prospect's attention with warm up conversation. It's not necessary to be the most outgoing person, everyone can participate in or initiate a conversation, but you do have to be interested and it is vital that the prospect be comfortable. Being a good conversationalist is a skill that can open unseen opportunities for you. To keep it interesting we must understand the ever-widening generation gaps and how to communicate with each on its own level.

Conversation is the face-to-face interaction that allows you to take in the prospect's inflections, emotions and physical gestures along with the spoken word. Conversation in large part enables the seller to take control of the process and also allows you to show respect to your prospect because you are interested and listening. Conversation is the glue that holds together the relationship between seller and prospect and is strategic to closing the sale. Needless to say, but you must be without biases, be impartial and be neutral when listening and effectively using your own body language, yep you have some too. Be very careful that you are not selling air, the warmup must produce evidence for leverage to use in your trial close and convictions during your presentation and to move a smooth close. In other words, what goes into your brain and what comes out of your mouth will determine what goes into your pocket.

Your prospect will want to know who he/she is dealing with and if you and your company have a history of success, they are also reading you. Keep it short and to the point and only discuss your awards when asked. Stories are important and everybody has a basket full to use, if you don't have a good story use someone else's. Some prospects will have limited time and in that situation there may little if any time to warm up, you should know this before the time and place is set for your presentation. Never be judgmental or stereotype a prospects personality or ability to pay, pre-judging is a huge mistake because that shabby, disheveled looking person may be very wealthy.

One excellent conversation can be about where the prospect stands in birth order with siblings and that information leads to a personality type which is very helpful. Patterns of thinking, behavior, and feelings can be related to birth order and to personality types. Personality may encompass nearly every aspect of our human experience and understanding personalities opens doors to conversation and ultimately to a relationship. Interest in this subject date back to the late 19th century and early 20th century when Dr. Alfred Adler suspected birth order may affect personality. The Birth Order Book by Dr. Kevin Leman is helpful in understanding personalities and how personalities affect our lives. The Birth Order Book should be mandatory study for all sales training.

SOCIAL STYLES: When I stated value in my presentation and wanted my prospect to pay close attention I would always say, "this part is very important to you." The prospect sitting across the table from me would lean in giving me clear signals about my product and my presentation. All we need to do is take the time to understand the messages and what is important to the prospect. Listen with your eyes as well as your ears and people will reveal a great deal of what they are thinking with their body language. When they lean in and make direct eye contact or use their hands to emphasize points you have made, they are communicating with you. Watch carefully and take notice of the prospects actions as well as reactions to identify what triggers their interest and if they are buying signals. This is where you engage with your prospects learning style.

The Driver: Comfortable in positions of power and control, authoritative, decisive and are the top five percent of achievers. Divers are direct and task oriented to achieve and will make quick decisions. They are active, forceful, determined, assertive, decisive, intelligent, impatient, independent and stubborn. They only want information that is relevant to the issue at hand. They are focused on effort, efficiency, effectiveness and goals accomplished for themselves and others. Drivers may not care for or about personal relationships.

Selling to the Driver: You must respect their time; warm up will need to be short as they will want to pass on small talk. Make your points clearly and quickly but be sure to stress value and how your product will satisfy the Drivers wants and needs, but you had better be able to back up your facts. The seller should project an image of confidence as well as strength and close quickly. Under stress Drivers may become autocratic. Show them value, show price, hand them the pen and say sign here.

The Analytical: Doctor, engineer, architect precision, business-like, rational, self-controlled, serious minded and are motivated by details and facts and the need to be right. They are accurate, precise, orderly, methodical, reserved and can be rigid but work well on strict timetables and are excellent problem solvers. They are organized, systematic, exact and logical and thrive on facts, data and history. The analytical will be more reserved in their interactions with people and social events and tend to disregard personal opinion in favor of facts.

Selling to the Analytical: Present in a logical but organized manner demonstrating results and show them guarantees or warrantees that reduce perceived risks. Analytical people are problem solvers who typically have slower reaction times and avoid conflict. Give them solutions or they will manifest a problem and you will not close easily if at all. The more you talk the more they will challenge your knowledge with questions you will have to answer and then they will stall to investigate for more information and avoid a buying decision. Tell the Analytical what he needs to know to make an informed buying decision and absolutely not one word more. When they question what you told them, tell it to them again.

The Amiable: Will be respectful, friendly, easy to present to, a willing listener, agreeable and supportive with a need for personal security. The seller can openly discuss the issues in a conversational format, they are softhearted and responsive. Amiables are team players that value relationships and are willing if not anxious to engage with people. Amiable people are relationship driven but need approval. They will focus on long-term problem solving.

Selling to the Amiable: Establish a personal relationship during warm up and discuss mutual interests and family. Collaborating is a valuable key to a commitment to buy. Use personal commitments and specific guarantees to demonstrate low risk solutions. The amiable prospect will avoid conflict at all cost and may agree with everything you say and back out at closing due to their need for personal security. A hard close will not work for you when selling to the Amiable.

The Expressive: Enthusiastic, emotional, spontaneous, talkative, opinionated, enjoy involvement, excitement and are social in interpersonal interaction but need approval. Be ready to make eye contact. They are willing to make their feelings and opinions known to others. They may at times appear to react impulsively but will openly show both positive and negative feelings.

Selling to the Expressive: They are idea-oriented and may use opinions and stories rather than facts and data, have little concern for routine, are focused on the future and have quick reaction times. Warm up is especially important as they are focused on people rather than on tasks. Present in a comfortable conversational manner with emphasis on value. A stressful or hard close will most likely be received as a personal attack on the prospect.

References:

I wish I Had Said That – Linda McCallister, PhD / Dr. McCallister breaks personality types into six types with advice how to communicate with each as well as how to deal with difficult people. This book should be part of all sales training and mandatory study for all sellers.
Personal Styles and Effective Performance - D.W. Merrill & R.H. Reid
Applications in Non-Verbal Communications - Ronald E. Riggio & Robert S. Feldman
Body Language – David Cohen
The 4 social styles - Jonathan Farrington
How to read customers accurately: Best practices - Ken Dooley
How to Listen and Double Your Influence with Others - *Brian Tracy*
The Birth Order Book: Dr. Kevin Leman

SALES PRESENTATION

● ● ● ● ●

A sales presentation is about helping the prospect solve a problem or reach a goal and it will survive or fail in the environment and within the relationship the seller creates. It must contain pertinent questions to establish evidence in order to transfer information and belief.
Sonny Culver, Sales Manager

● ● ● ● ●

Henry Ford in an attempt to streamline his production elected to paint all of his cars black, it was efficient and cost saving but customers who wanted an automobile of a different color went to his competitors. Mr. Ford's decision was efficient but not effective, but effective is where the money lives. This is not the time to get entangled between what is efficient vs. what is effective. Now is the time to trust your training and be effectively efficient.

The term sales pitch is repugnant to me, it sounds like a sucker punch to the prospects gut and anyone who wants to be a professional seller, certainly a Sales Craftsman should never use that term. The professional seller is not a con man and his product list does not include snake oil. Sales pitch is a negative statement that takes all the value away from a crafted and well-rehearsed professional transaction. In fact, what we want to do is establish a conversation based upon an exchange of information that leads to a signed contract. Along the way there will be a place for your proposal or presentation or better still an explanation of your value proposition that meets or exceeds the prospects wants and needs. A conversation is a relationship and relationships lead to long term satisfied customers. Why is it important to build a relationship with your prospect, because people will forget what you say or even what you do, but people never forget how you make them feel.

There is no replacement for a trusting relationship and a relationship with great clarity is of tremendous value to the customer.

Prospects today are overwhelmed with information and conditioning towards products and salespeople with much of it negative against the seller. From the prospects eye the questions are does the sellers presence, manner, clothing or car inspire confidence? Will this salesperson be able to offer an attractive solution and is that solution logical and is its good business? Even if the seller has what I need, do I want to buy from this salesperson? What can this seller do for me, what will it cost, when will it happen and when will the sales process end? These are the questions that the Sales is a Verb process is structured to overcome. The good news is that we perform miracles for people every day with our products and services, it's what we do.

What is a sales presentation, what is the purpose and how do I begin? The sales presentation is a systematic process to follow from appointment setting, arrival at the prospects home or business until exit. We begin by taking control, the prospect expects you to, then move smoothly through warm-up, wants and needs questions, probing deeper for hidden needs, offer a solution, qualify your company and the ability to exceed demand, close, warm down and leave on good terms with a signed contract, check in hand and at least one referral. The purpose for a sales presentation is to influence and motivate the prospect to understand how your product and the accompanying value proposition best meets their wants and needs, and to buy from you. What people want to talk about is themselves, their hopes, dreams, their situations, their problems and that is why you are at the table. You must have empathy because it is imperative to sell from the prospect's perspective. You must be impeccable with your words, have the courage to ask questions, speak with integrity and never make assumptions, because just like in physics, every action has a reaction. To do that you will need a well-rehearsed canned presentation without which you do not have a presentation. Without a well perfected presentation you are just another amateur who will soon be looking for work.

Most sellers will do a good job giving informational presentations but telling is not selling. The information you pass to the prospect in your presentation will be mostly disregarded because it contains little value to the prospect. Value is what you want to sell. If the prospect has a provider different than you, your sales presentation is about changing that behavior. Change is an alternative action for dissatisfaction and action is always preceded by dissatisfaction. But at the same time people procrastinate, are resistant to change and that is especially true when it is a behavioral change, so the seller must be positioned as the experienced and trusted advisor or counselor.

You begin every presentation with warm up conversation searching for common interest and common ground because people buy from people they like and who are like themselves. You must ask effective questions, probe and probe a little deeper. Then listen carefully, listen more than you talk while noting the wants and needs or what is important to the prospect. You want to know enough about the prospect expects to receive in order to offer a value filled presentation that defeats any opportunity for objections or stalls. If you aren't able to find and provide that kind of solution for your prospect it is a safe bet that your competitor will. In home, the best place for your presentation is seated at the kitchen table because that is where friends and family gather, it is a safe zone for the prospect. If beverage is offered take it.

What is on that table? Regardless of the physical items there are the prospects want and needs, anxiety, money, the prospects body language and emotions. Emotion sells, both yours and the prospect's but not without a convincing value propitiation as the main event in your presentation. Also, on that table are the tools you will use to provide the prospect with a value-based solution that makes you the best choice from whom to purchase. Keep in mind that there may be time frames for the transaction that you cannot control, but patience is the companion of wisdom. If you must ask personal questions be certain to inform the prospect early and ask for permission, it is good manners and may save the deal.

SALES IS A VERB SALES FORMULA

- Expect to win
- Preparation - gather information and materials, to make your presentation.
- Arrive at the point of sale in control and open a dialog.
- Warm-up – Establish rapport, trust and credibility, this is where the sale is made.
- Wants & Needs dialogue - Define the problem.
- Solutions dialogue – State a fact of evidence and describe the value and benefits you provide.
- Create a sense of urgency to sign with a chain of convictions.
- Qualify your company – But briefly, the company is not for sale.
- Resolve any objections.
- Close – Sign Contract.
- Collect Referrals.
- Warm down - This is how you keep the sale.

STEPS OF A SALES PRESENTATION:

Present in the **environment** you have created.

After opening your **presentation**, you will approach parts of your demonstration material that you are used to emphasize important value points, transfer belief or exhibit an advantage to your prospect. Develop your presentation points of interest and influence by alerting your prospects mind to receive a value, **"this part is very important to you."**

Qualify your company to be the best choice with a positioning statement, **Acme Company can take good care of this for you because**, and show a fact of value proving the strength of your company. Facts about your company and the follow-up description of benefits to meet the prospects needs have an emotional value. State the fact and then follow with the benefit, the two are tightly intertwined

There is no reason to waste precious time asking the prospect what they know about your company unless you are selling the company. Do not leave the value proposition laying idle on the table and jeopardize your close by glorifying your employer. Qualify your company to a logical advantage in your chain of convictions.

Give a **logical** reason for a decision-making reason to buy and tie it down with the evidence, people love the Acme service, product, quality or Acme can fix repair etc., **the advantage to you is.** Fact then value, is a sound logical statement leading to a logical decision to purchase. Logic is the justification to buy. Strengthen your presentation with bridge words, in bold letters, and a positioning statement to secure a commitment and build or your chain of convictions.

Follow-up with a **phycological** or comfort benefit, **the value to you is,** to relieve buyer stress and make you the obvious seller to buy from. State the phycological or good business reason to buy, Acme has a great warranty, a money back guarantee that is the best in our industry.

End each segment with a **trial close** asking for an opinion/conviction/commitment from the prospect and offering a motivation to buy. **In your opinion is** this the results, service etc., **that you expect to receive**. Tie it down using evidence discovered or supplied by the prospect.

A trial close is used to acquire a conviction. Tie it down with, "in your opinion are these the results you want." There are many adaptations, but never use the term, "<u>don't you think or agree</u>." That is an offensive manipulation leading the prospect to believe he or she is being told how to think and is likely a short-term cancelation, never use the phrase, "<u>don't you</u>." Create value during each transition of your presentation and earn the right to take the next step. Go from conviction to conviction which is in reality is a commitment to buy given by the prospect.

Objections at this point are favorable to you, put it to bed early.

Move to the next segment of your presentation and repeat the steps.

Bridge words, positioning and alert statements, in upper case below, put muscle into your presentation and are used to secure a commitment and build on your chain of convictions. The idea is to connect clauses or sentences with flexibility, bridge smoothly and create narrative flow to connect separate ideas with a relationship. The reason for using bridge words or statements in transition is that they help bring two ideas together to gain coherence, sum up a conclusion and to make the most desirable contract for a side.

- Alert for attention - **This Part Is Very Important to You**, leads to a position statement
- Make a positioning statement - Acme can supply, repair, or service **"Because"** State a logical reason for decision.
- **"The Advantage,"** to you is that Acme's service, product is or can. Give a phycological benefit - **The Value to You Is,"** Acme's warranty, guarantee
- Trial close and conviction - **"In Your Opinion,"** you are looking for a positive answer or opinion that leaves the prospect feeling in control, evidence will always defeat disbelief.
- Move to the next segment or close

Example: This part is very important to you, the Sales is a Verb process has guided other successful sellers to higher earnings and the technique only takes practice to master and put into action. **The Value of Sales is a Verb to you** is that your workload will be become orderly, and your income will increase because you are spending more time selling. **The advantage to you** is that anyone who can sell at a higher level will never need to look for work because good jobs will look for you. **In your opinion do these results meet your expectations**. Collect the conviction, add it to your chain of convictions and transition to the next segment, then repeat the process

This part is very important to you, use any electronic device and practice every part of your presentation and close until you can't get it wrong, **because every presentation has a life or death of its own.**

Selling Value: What is a value proposition? A value proposition is a clear and measurable position statement, mental picture, that offers a logical, tangible economic or personal value to the prospect for purchasing your product or service. You have no control over your competition regardless of what you sell or to whom you may sell. Low-ball pricing is always going to be there, it is not to be feared but to be overcome so let's consider that. Unless you are bidding on a government contract price is not the primary factor. You can't compete on price alone because only bankers and loan sharks successfully sell money. What you have is a product or service that you are proud to sell, and your presentation is structured to offer a good business decision and the logical choice for your prospect. Don't be afraid to compare your proposition against your competitor.

Never use the words dollars, price or cost because those words distract from value. In the absence of value every sale becomes a contest with the customer about price. Only after demonstrating the best value deal that you can, do we discuss investment. Do your value presentation well and there should be little if any price resistance or buyer's remorse after the sale. Although price is a factor in every sale it is seldom the primary factor. In our modern environment the seller may feel pressured to offer discounts and concessions in order to close the sale. If price becomes a factor it is because the seller failed to demonstrate sufficient investment value for the product or service over price. If you find yourself in that situation you will need to have practiced your negotiating skills. Value is always easier to sell than price.

How do we support a higher price for our product? Easy, sell value. An investment value today is logical while cost for the unknown is out of pocket and probably a lifetime of misery. Be competent, everyone appreciates the highest quality of product and service which equals value. People buy a product with the expectation of the results from that purchase, hence value. Value stimulates the prospects thinking to anticipate enjoying the benefit of that desired value. When the prospect perceives he will get more benefit from the investment than from the price, all you need to do is say sign here and then shut your mouth. The more you focus on value the less important price becomes. The seller who sells value is more confident and feels less pressure to lower the price even against aggressive demands.

VALUE Vs PRICE: There must be something of value in the purchase for the prospect to buy from you. Value is your secret weapon and it's about what's in it for the prospect, and that value perception is a huge wedge between you, price and the competition. Value gives life to the decision to purchase from you. Likability and friendships are important but being likable is not enough motivation to separate the prospect from their money unless there is something of economic value. What you bring to the table must be so worthwhile that the prospect is willing to pay for it. Creating an economic value for the prospect will create a biased preference to purchase from you, plus you won't have to deal with price issues. You can create a biased preference when your value creates a greater economic impact and you can do that at a higher price. Always ask YES questions and you will get YES answers. May we look at the other proposal, just to see if there are any difference that will benefit you? If we can find a greater value for your money, wouldn't it be worth a little more? All of your communications with the prospect must be relevant to the wants and needs you have uncovered, stay focused on the prospect's priorities, your job is to become the trusted value resource. Author Stephen R. Covey said, "The main thing is to keep the main thing the main thing.'

Selling to Friends or Family: Should you have the good fortune to present to family or a friend remember it is strictly business, never disrespect someone close to you by giving the short version presentation. Give them the best you have; they will be impressed and tell others.

You will get all you want in life if you help enough other people get what they want.
Zig Zigler, American author, salesman, and motivational speaker

CLOSING THE SALE

● ● ● ● ●

You can close more business in two months
by being interested in other people
than you can in two years trying to get people interested in you.
Dale Carnegie, American writer and lecturer

● ● ● ● ●

Close is the summation of your presentation and should arrive to its natural conclusion where you get what you are worth, a signed contract, money in hand and at least one referral. The secret to closing is to know when to close but by its nature is always aggressive.

The best closing technique is to follow the Sales is a Verb presentation procedure diligently and prevent your prospect from becoming indecisive or needing to stall or think it over. However, even though the earth is round it does have a few bumps. If you run into a bump there will be signals to what additional close devices you may need to use.

Sales Craftsman do not introduce dollars into their presentation or at close because it is guaranteed to cause hesitation to buy. Investment is a better phycological term than cost or price or dollars and is more logically sound. An investment is good and ongoing, while dollars are immediately out of pocket and probably an eternity of misery. If you have a financing option available, it is best to offer three investment plans rather than drop a large number on the prospect. If the prospect asks for the total price give them the investment, the prospects may want to crow a little and pay cash but that is their decision, always offer financing first. Either way you still have payment options to discuss without negotiating the investment. The prospect may stall to get a lower payment, agree with them and move to extended terms and the possibility of a down payment or perhaps alternative financing.

High pressure tactics, when obvious, will almost always cause the prospect to resist and even if the prospect does sign your contract it may be short term and canceled. But to say I don't believe in a hard close is both amateur and sophomoric. The meek seller may inherit the earth, but they will be in poverty when it happens. We are always on the offensive, consequently all closes are aggressive, but the aggression must be intelligent and subtle. The reason for an aggressive close is twofold, one, prospects tends to hesitate or procrastinate especially if they are unfamiliar with the product, service or company. Two, your time is valuable because the time you spend selling is tied to your income, it is certainly cliché but for you time is money.

There are hundreds if not thousands of different close techniques and phrases, some simple and some more complicated but each one requires a decision to buy from the prospect. You want to make the buying decision simple and as easy as a minor decision, but you must do it with integrity. I wish it were possible to note each and every one and perhaps some application but then only a power lifter could carry this book home. Here are a few of the most common close phrases and techniques.

The Sales is a Verb Close Should Always be Your 1st Close - Transfer belief and confidence at close buy smoothly passing the service contract to in front of your prospect and hand the prospect a pen. Now, tie the sale down with this statement, **"and we will do a good job for you."** Do not add to or take away, just say it with a sincere tone and expression. This is a great close and no matter what happens next the prospect has a pen in hand and the contract is in the right place to be signed.

Feel, Felt, Found Close - "I understand how you feel" – shows empty and that you can relate, "others have felt that way" – The thought is common, but the situation can change. "What they found was doing X was that Y happened even though they paid a little more they saved a lot more".

Example: "I understand how you **feel** others have said that. One of my best customers **felt** that way initially, but when they looked at our benefits, they **found** that they saved more money by purchasing from Acme.

We all want others to be sensitive to and understand us or our position and it isn't always easy for us, but we can make it easy for the prospect. The feel felt and found statements can be a strong method to overcome price resistance. "I understand how you feel." "Other customers have felt that way but found this is the best option." After agreeing with the prospect restate your value proposition to align the prospects objectives and reassert priorities. When we acknowledge how our prospect feels we make the statement that we have listened to him or her and understand their position. The felt statement diminishes the objection as a reason not to do business with you. The found statement outlines clearly how customers were rewarded for choosing your product or service. Feel, felt, found used together is a great way to get your prospect to see past the objection and be justified to purchase from you without adding anxiety but rather to release it.

Reverse Close – That may be to very reason you should do business with Acme Company.

Sharp or Right Angle Close – Used for the prospect hesitating to make a change for seemingly no reason, "I know you want to go forward or to do it and set a date," or some variation.

Alternative Close – Would you like to begin on Tuesday or Friday? It is sold so when do you want it?

Inducement Close – Offering a gift or prize, be sure you can deliver or there is trouble ahead.

Porcupine Close – Ignore signals and describe the prospects pleasure with the product or service.

Instructive Choice: Sign your approval here, make your check payable to, we can start tomorrow.

The Takeaway Close – If the prospect is struggling to say yes it may be due to costs or some other factor, offer to take away one or more features to make the deal a more appealing investment. You can always come down on the amount of service or product offered.

Impending Doom Close - Can be used if in fact an emergency exists or if a sharp price increase is scheduled.

Ben Franklin Close - A summary of Pros and Cons to prove purchasing from you is the best decision. Time consuming but if you use this one be certain your offer is superior to the adversarial company because minor differences do not sway most prospects.

Visualization Close - Visualizing the end results and full impact of the purchase. Sales is about that wonderful thing that is about to happen.

Hidden Authority Close - Some products and services are sold using the hidden authority technique, car dealerships use it effectively. The seller knowing that a reduction of price is available comes to an agreed purchase amount with the prospect. Seller tells the prospect that he can call his boss, who is very busy, but the deal must be solid for the seller to make the call. The seller is now working for the buyer, the boss will ask questions about the job and the give approval. Without management questioning the deal it can take on the appearance of a scam or it could be a bad deal for the company.

How do you decide which closing phrases and technique are the best to use? Verbal statements and body language cues are your friend if you know how to use them, but you must be focused on the prospect. If the prospect's voice is warm and friendly or excited, your close presentation is likely going in the right direction. But if your prospects voice is curt, short or irritated or perhaps showing anxiety, these are clear signals to change up on your approach. The same is true for body language. Eye contact, the prospects head tilting forward towards you and an engaged posture are very good signs that you're being positively received. Leaning back in his chair with arms crossed are two signs that you and the prospect are not on friendly ground. If the seller wavers so will the prospect, time to reassess your strategy and start at a different level.

Personality types, birth order and the clues they afford us are of no less importance. If you haven't already taken a course on how to read different personality types and the best approach to gain the prospects confidence and close sales, do it now. Personality types are not an exact science because every person is unique and will respond differently based on culture, conditioning and life experiences. However, there are personality frameworks that can be used to guide the sales process. Four types, discussed in the Read the Prospect section are driver, analytical, amiable and expressive. If you use the popular DISC model the four personality types are: dominant, inspiring, supportive and cautious. Description is irrelevant but learning to identify personalities and how to close each personally type is imperative for the Sales Craftsman. You can make money at a day job, but wealth comes from doing your homework, learn to read your prospects.

Buyers today are tech savvy and much better informed than prospects were in the past. They will have enough data to help them through the research and evaluation phases of the product or service they want. Prospects today are buying products and services online and that includes big ticket items like homes and automobiles. As prospects enter the formal phase of buying, they usually know what problems they are trying to solve and are acquainted with their options and solutions. They will also know about how much money they are willing to spend for their purchase. All of this makes a huge difference for the seller at close. Handled by offering fact followed by a value benefit and conviction from a well-developed relationship and established creditability will make you the logical choice when you ask for the sale.

SOME THINGS TO DO:

Be confident in yourself and always assume the customer will buy. The Sales Craftsman who confidently ask for the business will get more signed contracts than those who are hesitant or uncertain. Keep it simple, be bold, ask clearly and sincerely with the confidence that you have offered the very best value and benefits for your prospects wants and needs.

An honest objection is a positive buying signal, answer it and close on it.

Use the prospects name during the presentation and be absolutely certain to pronounce it correctly. Getting it right indicates interest in the prospect, otherwise a mispronounced name can be received as an insult. Respect proves the seller is working for the prospect.

Learn all that you can about the prospect and find common ground as the basis for a strong relationship.

Do not speak after you ask the prospect to buy because the next person to speak loses.

SOME THINGS NOT TO DO:

Never attack the prospects current course of action or a competitor even if the prospect brings up negative language. Say something passive like, I've heard that, but I would rather talk about what my company can do for you. Attacking a competitor may be received as a personal attack on the prospect.

Always be closing is lame advice that is completely ineffective in the environment we live in today. The Craftsman has no need to push the prospect hard and constantly asking them to buy. That way will not get the contract signed but it will get you a bad name.

What will it take to earn your business today or what will it take to get you to buy is begging the prospect to seek a price reduction and will not purchase otherwise at this point? This technique works well only for those who enjoy working for low wages or worse, working for free.

Some sellers will become angry when the prospect refuses the sale because they are desperate. Desperation to sell leads to angry desperation and the prospect can smell it. They also smell price reduction which blocks value out of the conversation. Not only will the prospect not buy but he will tell others to beware. A contract signed with fear of anger is done so at the cost of the company and sellers reputation. If management becomes aware that the seller uses this method the contract must be declined with apology to the customer.

HANDELING STALLS: The stall is an emotional barrier that prevents the prospect from buying. When you have a stall, it is time to become the curious student and not the long-winded expert.

Typical stalls are: We want to think about it or sometimes pray about it. We don't have the money, or we can't afford that, yet you were invited to make a presentation for this sale. If you have a financing option the deal is not dead, you just have to find an acceptable payment plan. I am already well covered with insurance, but still here you are across the table. I'm just looking, is what we all say at the auto dealership before we drop a bundle of cash. Price is not an objection but a stall for time, price will always stimulate suspicion if not well qualified with a conviction of value for the prospect.

True Story: The seller was a man with an endless line of dominate chatter going nowhere and he was a heavy smoker. You know him. His presentation was hard and fast without regard to the prospects time, wants or needs. All this seller understood was to hit hard and fast until the prospect would give in under the pressure and sign the contract. But this prospect had a very effective stall, "we have to pray about it." Never daunted the seller said "that's OK I'll step outside for a smoke and when you finish call me in." Shortly the door opened and the seller's briefcase along with all of his sales material came sailing into the yard. Perhaps there was Devine intervention but had seller had an effective warm-up and used his power of observation about the prospect and the surroundings, even as unprofessional as he was that sale could have closed. Instead, he worked for free.

There may be valid reasons for prospects to stall or put off making a purchase decision. If you find yourself in a stall situation you must find clarification for the stall because there is an unknown situation or hidden reality and until you identify that reality you have no avenue to overcome it. In a stall situation ask open ended who, what, when, where questions and do not interrupt the answer. Yes or no questions will get you short closed ended answers and a dialog shut down; you have nowhere to lead the conversation at that point.

Typically stalls have one thing in common, the prospect has stalled to prevent signing your contract because the seller hasn't convinced the prospect of the value proposition. Seller didn't ask for needed commitments and/or seller didn't build a consensus or a trusting relationship. In short, the seller's close preparation was faulty because the seller didn't follow the sales process. There is no part of your presentation more important than a relationship building warmup and a compelling value proposition followed by a chain of convictions to prevent and overcome the stall. The best way to deal with a stalled opportunity is to follow the Sales Is A Verb formula and not allow the stall surface in the first place.

HANDLING OBJECTIONS: An objection is the much the same as a stall because the decision to purchase is on hold, but objections are easier to deal with and overcome. Every prospect will be different, and that difference requires flexibility and adaptability when dealing with objections. An objection is a reason for disagreeing, opposition to a point or even a challenge. If the objection is to a fact or value, it can be a good thing. How you deal with your options for objections is the test of how you perform as a professional salesperson and graduate to Craftsman.

"What if "questions and "but" statements are not objections, they are clarification questions, verify the question or statement before replying, then answer with pinpoint accuracy and validate the value.

There are two types of objection to deal with: the first is simply a misunderstanding that you can set straight with an explanation and an apologize. The second is a concern of a more important nature that you must resolve.

THE STEPS TO OBJECTION RESOLUTION:

Listen with sincere interest to the objection.
Feed the objection back by restating the objection.
Question the objection, look for the basis of the concern.
Answer it with confidence
Confirm your answer.
By the way, is a good transition to the next topic.

Attentive Listening: Let's talk about listening because it is not the same as hearing. Listening is the active mental absorption of speech, ideas and thoughts while hearing is inactive, passive and possibly self-absorbed. When salespeople are excellent listeners, prospects and customers feel comfortable and secure and believe they can trust the seller, they talk. Listening also gives the seller time to think about the objection and develop a strategy to satisfy the prospects end expectation. Attentive listening is a self-esteem booster for the prospect and lowers stress and price resistance, plus listening is a good business practice. Listen carefully to the objection's emotion and to the prospects body language because there are buying signals clearly on display.

Feedback: Restate the prospects objection in your own words to confirm accuracy. You want the prospect to hear the objection as it was spoken to you. Pull the prospects natural flow towards you and look for buying signals. Humor is helpful as long as the prospect is not the target.

Question the objection: Where it is appropriate ask a question to verify the objection and the basis for or reasoning for the objection. Do not ask why questions, you do not want to put the prospect in a defensive posture. You are seeking to find what is hidden behind the objection and read between the lines.

Answer the objection: No matter how much you want to talk, the level of your product knowledge your tenure or experience, careful listening and clarification are your finest sales tools. Answer the objection with honesty and sincerity but have a good, logical business answer.

Confirm your answer: You may want to repeat the answer for clarification. There should be a since of urgency to buy after you satisfy the objection, move to close.

By the way: Is an excellent way to move away from the objection and change the cognitive frame, move on to the next segment or to simply change gears.

For their own reason's buyers may not tell you if there is a hidden need and may try to mask it. You must make eye contact and be the curious student to uncover and bring the issue into the open before you can satisfy whatever that need may be. Be quiet, nodding to let your body language speak in agreement, and let the prospect get their entire point across before you say anything. Lean forward looking at the prospect to show you are interested and concentrating on what is important to him or her.

INTERNATIONAL MARKETS AND CUSTOMERS:

Selling in an international market or to foreign nationals even if the prospects are local, is much different than here in the U.S. because customs and traditions vary widely. A thumbs up, for example, means all good in America but may be an insult in some other country. If you should have the lucrative opportunity to sell in the international market be sure to do your homework before first contact.

The Golden Rule of Listening: *It's possible to say too much.*
It's rarely possible to listen too much.
How to Listen and Double Your Influence
with Others, by Brian Tracy

SALES MANAGEMENT

● ● ● ● ●

"Fortune favors the bold." Publius Vergilius Maro (Virgil) Roman poet

● ● ● ● ●

So, you want to be a Sales Manager, chaos is going to be your new normal. Now you get to deal with a multitude of wayward personalities, some of which you will swear should be institutionalized in a place with bars and locks.

Best of all they will have feelings, oh yes everyone has feelings that you are expected to step politely around. If you are sensitive to those feelings, they will grow and grow bigger until there is no way to move around those folks without hurting at least one feeling. Some of your sales staff will never hear a single word you say because they are only interested in their reply, and they will manage to cause a multitude of problems with/for staff and customers. They will argue endlessly because they do not respect you, the customer or themselves. Those are the same ones who lead the parking lot meetings to work against you and the company that pays them. They will be the same people bringing in more revenue than other sales staff, but they manage to cripple the sales team and cause morale problems with other staff members, fire them. There will be drama queens who are dishonest with you and lie endlessly; they come in all shapes and sizes. If you are successful and bring in more revenue than the front office is accustomed to handling, they will hate you for taking away their phone and Internet shopping time. Not only will they hate you through their smiles, but they will also do everything they can to slow down your efforts. As an added perk they will attack your salespeople hoping to cause turn over for you.

Should these people be tenured under a long-time manager, they will be sacred cows, and you are not. And as a bonus, the Human Resources Department will not be your friend. If you are really successful, your less successful peers will set out mine fields and you are the bomb tech.

Anyone can wear the title of manager, but there is a critical shortage of capable management. There are many reasons for that, poor selection and poor training are obvious but, in my view, the poorest is the person who puts himself first in any situation. Tragically, when the self-centered selfish person reaches middle management or a senior position, as they often do in any business, military or political position, every day becomes a crisis, and it is all your fault. Management is about responsibility and service to others and when we practice everyone but me first the personal rewards are overwhelmingly good. The workload will be heavy in startup and turnaround situations, but respect yourself and do it anyway, doer's get more done.

We had sales contest between offices with the losing branch office paying the dinner bill for the winning branch office sales staff and their spouses. The ticket for those meals and beverage looked like the national debt which will always excite the bean counters at corporate. But the wives enjoyed a paid evening out and women being women each got a new outfit to wear. They also helped me keep Bubba off the coach and in the field. Peers, several in much larger cities and therefore with a greater base of prospects, complained to the Region Manager that it was unfair for us to win all the time and of course we must be cheating in some way. The RM decided to have region wide contest and branches were teamed, more for his optics than for region performance. He effectively did away with the dinner expense and replaced it with trinkets. You can see where this is going. The RM tried every combination of offices to pair us with, but we always won. In my last sales contest, I was paired with two non-productive offices, one managed by a Manager Trainee. I called and asked those managers if they wanted to win, they both said yes but I knew one could not and the other would not help.

By phone I took over the sales operations of both offices and addressed each seller on an individual basis to establish strategy, for them there was energy in the air, perhaps for the first time. The sales staffs of those two offices reported to me from early to late and posted the leader board together with us by speakerphone. We did not win by much, but we won head to head honest and fair. Of the hundreds of sales events I was involved in, I have never lost a sales contest. We were not a team that followed history, we were a team that made history. The point of this is that **Winners focus on winning while losers focus on winners.**

You are probably asking yourself why would anyone work in that environment? The answer is because Sales Management is the best job and the most fun you can have and still get paid to do it. I was focused on a process of providing a great service value for our customers and developing my staff into a strong professional unit, even as I learned. At a time when the average salesperson in that company earned 35K annually, I had people earning over 100k and no one earning under 60K. Three of the original eight sales staff members went on to be successfully self-employed in that industry while others continue to be top producers enjoying higher income and benefits. None of what you have just read above is particularly negative, but it is part and parcel of negotiating life in the fast lane. Accept the challenge; focus on winning and winning it all. I had so much fun that some days I would have worked without pay, never say that to the boss.

THE SPEED OF THE LEADER IS
THE SPEED OF THE PACK:

There is a time to be cavalier and a time to be humble. Cavalier is a good tool when you are trying to build a winning team or win a sales contest because the energy is contagious but will be seen as arrogance when things are going well, and you are a winner. The overly cavalier manager will make powerful enemies because they cannot keep up. Humble winners who are willing to share ideas and or methods build strong networks of followers, even if they are not in your chain of authority. There will be others, usually peers, and the know it all bunch, who listen politely during meetings but hang on to their failure and mediocrity. Many times, during meetings, held by middle management and often observed by senior management, I was asked to speak concerning how to improve sales and yet those who did not attain their budgeted revenue goals failed to adopt any strategy other than just getting by. It was obvious that middle management did not have the resolve to insist upon excellence and/or feared the budgeted increase in revenue for the coming year. Fear of revenue, especially when it is easy to acquire is foolish. In any event people were allowed or perhaps even encouraged to fail. Weak managers never get to the moral center of management but are often promoted above those who are more capable of leading because they are likable or better equipped to patronize.

THE MORNING SUCCESS RITUAL: There are many tasks to perform early every day, much of it will be piled on your desk waiting to be read, be signed or delegated. But nothing is more important than meeting with the team as a group and one on one. All of our electronic awareness is wonderful stuff, but it cannot replace a positive atmosphere or selective training and the team building of the morning meeting. Tell admin to take a message, there are to be no interruptions, EVER. Collect the new business, inspect it for accuracy and look at the seller's plan for today and inspect lead production. If the seller doesn't have a plan for today or if you need to address a negative disposition, that is why you are there. It is dishonorable to allow someone to fail because you did not help.

Each seller must individually post the Leader Board in a morning meeting ritual is extremely important for the competitive spirit of the team and an excellent way to build morale. Each seller should have posted a sales and referral commitment on the first day of the month, you can expect what you inspect, you will only get what you ask for.

I am aware that some companies have chosen to stop posting a Leader Board because whiney people had hurt feelings. What? No discipline results in failure to comply, overcome feelings with discipline. Once again: It is a dishonorable to allow someone to fail because you did not help.

LEAD PRODUCTION: Most organizations have defined marketing and advertising programs for continuous lead generation. These programs are constructed at the corporate and sometimes local market levels to assist sellers and sales managers to meet and exceeding revenue objectives. Procedural guidelines and expectation levels for the accurate and timely disposition of leads is essential to correctly assess the quality of those programs because each lead is both expensive and valuable.

Review of team status on an on-going basis is necessary to ensure that all associates are within required benchmarks and when appropriate, take the necessary corrective action for those who fail to meet minimum standards. Sellers must be required to meet specific guidelines in order to ensure their continued participation in company lead programs. Any seller that fails to meet the minimum standards set forth will normally be removed from participation in company sponsored lead programs and may be subject to disciplinary action up to and including termination of employment.

Disposition rates of lead generation should always be above 90% closed. A pending lead requires the seller to provide additional detailed status on the outcome of the lead and the next scheduled appointment and the status, steps that are necessary to complete the sales cycle.

Sellers are expected to utilize company tools and personal skills to expand presence in the local market. Everyone in the office, regardless of title, is in sales and should generate referral leads.

These are a few factors to inspect but are not limited to:

Experience and attitude
Effective lead closure
Revenue production by seller
Closing Ratio, Referral Skills
Lead Disposition Ratio (Close Percentage 90 or better)
Seller schedule, daily activity and availability
(Human Resources will tell you that attitude is not measurable, and that is a bunch of meadow muffins.)

COMMUNICATIONS: Are you a great communicator? Communicating clearly and taking responsibility for the other person understanding of what you say will benefit your leadership and extend to better communications from seller to prospect. If you do not communicate effectively, your staff has a confusing direction, and your goals have no value no matter how clear they may be to you. Failure to communicate clearly up will cause frustration for you and your supervisor. Communicating up is more difficult for various reasons but Boss time is a reality to be dealt with. Whether your message is unclear, or the supervisor isn't capable understanding does not matter, your success is balanced by how well the person listening is able to consume your message in the most positive manner.

Rule of thumb: It is the responsibility of the speaker to ensure that the listener clearly understands the definition and content of the message. One of the secrets to having happy employees is their having trust in communicating with you. Trust is the first order of communicating in any direction but if you are perceived as untrustworthy or self-serving to the point of patronizing, no matter what your message it will be suspect. Friendly communications are better than assertive language, build a relationship because the listener is interesting, focus individual attention on the listener and make sure everything about you sends the right message.

DISCIPLINE: Self-discipline is a matter of self-respect that leads to being respected by others. Self-discipline is the execution of will power over your basic desires and reactions. We are equally responsible for our actions, our reactions and the resulting consequences. Self-discipline is what supports honesty and moral courage and is a major key to success. Work on self-discipline every day in order to set the example for how people around you should conduct themselves.

Discipline is the practice of training people to obey a set of rules or a code of behavior. The controlled behavior resulting from discipline is necessary to maintain focus on the plan and is a strong motivator when fairly and evenly applied. Discipline begins on day one as is expected. The kind of discipline administered is what divides great managers or mediocrity to failure. Business is not a conflict although conflicts can arise to test your vision and stamina. More often than not those problems are turf wars between service and sales, but it doesn't require the Wisdom of Solomon to maintain order and improve relationships. Give those people projects to work on together and build a community instead of kingdoms. Evaluate them and require them to write an evaluation of their cooperative projects, working together builds unit cohesion and strong integrity.

> *"Business is an ecosystem, not a battlefield, and that our employees are not our children, but they are our peers." Geoffrey James of Inc. Magazine*

BUSINESS PLANNING

• • • • •

"Planning is a process of choosing among those many options. If we do not choose to plan, then we choose to have others plan for us."
Richard I. Winwood COO Franklin-Covey

• • • • •

If you haven't written a business plan or perhaps any type of written plan it can be a difficult task learning a new skill. Old habits are hard to break and starting to plan requires strong focus and attention to detail but on the other hand momentum will come from taking small steps.

Online or otherwise you may purchase software that can be tailored to your market or use your P & L Statement as a guide. Your business plan will serve as a road map guiding your operation towards success. When your people know what to do and have a map to get there the energy and commitment will produce excellent results.

Write a detailed plan, include management staff and ask for their ideas and opinions. Share your business plan and vision with your all levels of staff in an office meeting with real food and beverage. Distribute and explain it to your staff, ask them to buy in and you will have arranged your own good luck.

Business plans and budgeting require management to see the long-term big picture, but long-term success is the results of short-term what did you do today actions of the small picture. Business planning is the act of bringing the future into the present by forecasting revenue and expenses in order that specific objectives may be managed. The best business plans are straightforward documents that spell out the who, what, when, where, why, how much and are the difference between

98

thriving and attempting to survive. A business plan is a list of actions arranged in a desired sequence to maintain focus on the momentum of each department and is thought likely to achieve an objective. The end result of your plan will be affected by how you arrange and manipulate the ingredients of your Business Plan for a predictable ending. A goal without a plan is merely hope without a strategy.

Executive Summary: Include every level of management involved in plan implementation and involve them in the process. Everyone, sales, service or management must know their numbers in order to know where they stand in relation to success of the plan. If you don't know your numbers, you don't know your business.

Mission: For your business and employees to perform at the highest level everyone needs a clear vision of what the business stands for, where it is going and how will we get there. What is your competitive edge?

Objectives: Budgeted revenue acquisition and customer retention numbers are a good place to start. That which is not measured will have no value.

Sales Plan: Budgeted revenue acquisition and personnel are addressed here. Provide sales incentives to sales staff to meet sales goals. Great incentives equal great revenue increases.

Advertising Plan & Marketing Plan: Your company may have a department dedicated to production in these areas, but you can still do things on a local level to push prospect and revenue acquisition. Look for the 20 percent of activities that account for 80 percent of your results.

Service Plan: If you do not have a detailed plan on how customers are to be serviced' you will soon have no customers to serve. Establish positive relationships with current and new customers. Service must be a part of prospect acquisition and repeat customer revenues.

Strategy and Implementation: The best strategy is to include everyone in formulating your business plan. Create agreements and expectations, if you do that implementation should be easy. You may want to formulate plans to acquire new products or territory, it doesn't matter but sharing and starting to take action does matter positively.

Commitment: Commitment is the glue that makes the difference between success and failure.

"By Failing to prepare, you are preparing to fail."
Benjamin Franklin, American Founding Father

MARKETING & ADVERTISING PLANNING

●　●　●　●　●

Webster: Advertising
Is act or practice of calling public attention to one's product,
service, need, etc., especially by paid announcements in newspapers
and magazines, over radio or television on billboards, etc.

Webster: Marketing
Is the activity, set of institutions, and processes for creating,
communicating, delivering, and exchanging offerings that
have value for customers, clients, partners, and society at
large. Making people aware of a company's products, making
sure that the products are available to be bought, etc.

Definition for the rest of us:
Marketing and Advertising are the same thing only different.

●　●　●　●　●

Advertising includes the selling and delivering of products to consumers or businesses. If your company has an in-house Advertising Department you will likely have to apply for permission for any local advertising expense and the answer is always no.

Marketing refers to activities undertaken by a company to promote the buying or selling of a product or service. If your company has an in-house Marketing department, they may devise burdensome nonproductive programs doomed for failure and the failure will be your fault. But there are a great many things you can do to build community awareness and relationships that can attract a large number of prospects doing small things on a local level.

Marketing and Advertising are naked without Public Relations. Ads and commercials or any other vehicle are no substitute for solid communications that build relationships. An idea is useless without a suitable voice to present it, in the field the voice is the seller. On an individual basis two thirds of your marketing is the seller's personal brand, that means what other people are saying about you and what people are telling other people about you. Eighty percent of adults dismiss advertising but believe word of mouth. The customer is the marketer and you are the brand, polish your brand.

Online marketing includes a myriad of advertising opportunities, such as:

Local website advertising including Facebook, Twitter, Craigslist and similar sites.

Join the Chamber of Commerce; most chapters have websites that provide listings of local businesses.

Create and maintain a professional website outlining descriptions of your business.

Email newsletters can be useful for keeping in touch with existing customers and prospecting.

Cold calling by phone or in person is no one's favorite but it can be surprisingly effective. Vehicle decals or magnetic stickers turn your vehicle into mobile billboard gives you excellent exposure.

Door Hangers are cheap to produce and distribute. If you follow-up there will be sales.

Industrial Shows, Home Shows, County Fairs and Shopping Mall Shows are my favorite way to market. In my city there are two large events each March and we were always there. I rented two adjoining booths and we displayed every product we sold with a logoed wooden ballot box between the tables for lead collection. The feature was a mid-price range propane grill holding a sign saying Register to win. Do not allow chairs because every person passing by must be greeted and asked, "did you register for the grill." The register slip had our services listed along with name, address and phone number of the prospect. You must be aggressive but if you do this as well, in a mid-sized city, you can expect in excess to three thousand leads per event. My sellers earned very good money and turnover was not an issue but if I had to add to the sales staff the new seller had someone to call who had expressed an interest to purchase at least one of our products.

Recruit every day because Murphy is trolling your team.

> **"Have a bias towards action – let's see something happen now. You can break that big plan into small steps and take the first step right away."**
> **Indira Gandhi, Prime Minister of India**

SALES PLANNING

● ● ● ● ●

"The Will to Win Is Nothing Without the Will to Prepare."
Zig Ziglar. "Ziglar on Selling."

● ● ● ● ●

Your sales plan is important because it directly relates to the first rule of business, which is to PROTECT THE INVESTMENT. Therefore, those responsible for bringing in the revenue that protects if not guards the investment must have special attention. Numbers will need to be your first concern in order to establish how many sellers will be needed to gain budgeted revenue. More than the bottom line measures your success, but the bottom line is what keeps you employed.

Make your sales plan a campaign with action steps that connect every avenue that will produce prospects and revenue. You can't afford to miss any opportunity that will get more prospects and closed sales so keep yourself organized and set clear goals that will stretch your team's abilities, and when you accomplish a goal reset and reach farther. Target your prospects and have a plan to engage them with value that gains the trust of your staff first and then the prospect. To do that you will need a well-defined sales revenue plan and a strong sales training plan that targets growth but not one set in stone, you must be prepared to adapt daily if need be. When necessary changing your action steps to a different approach will be necessary to yield different results.

Your sales training plan, different from product training, must touch every stage of the sales cycle, specifically prospecting and building a pipeline with opportunities for success and increased revenue, referrals, introductions, presentation and closing. The process must include high-value discovery questions to get the wants and needs information you require to offer a value proposition to the prospect. Then there must be practice and more practice until every part works perfectly.

The first Super Bowl was won by the Green Bay Packers who perfected the Packer sweep. Coach Lombardi ran this formation for wind sprints, he ran it over and over and it was the first and last formation of every practice. Everyone knew the Packers were going to run that play but it was so smooth and powerful that no one could stop it, the same rule applies in sales. The sales plan must also include sales events to keep your sales team and support associates engaged. You must audit your sales plan on a monthly, perhaps weekly basis depending upon your success against budgeted and actual revenue capture.

Recruit every day because Murphy is trolling your team.

**"If you don't know where you are going,
you'll end up someplace else."
"Yogi" Berra, Major League Baseball
Catcher, Manager and Coach**

SERVICE PLANNING

• • • • •

"For tomorrow belongs to the people who prepare for it today."
African Proverb

• • • • •

Service is a duty to someone who has paid you to perform certain functions and actions. The service relationship you develop with your customers will decide your retention rates and revenue capture as well as your longevity in whatever position you hold.

In the same manner as your sales plan service directly relates to the first rule of business, which is to PROTECT THE INVESTMENT. Therefore, the service people responsible for bringing in the revenue and keeping cancellations low must also have special attention. Numbers will need to be your first concern in order to establish how many service people will be needed to gain budgeted revenue and customer retention.

Service people will have a very different personality from sellers but with a little couching they can add to their income and help capture sales revenue. Often the service person will have more credibility with customers than sellers so there is no reason not to take advantage of their abilities. It helps to build team effort and team morale if you have a budget for service department sales. Start small with a number of sales rather than a dollar amount but it needs to be voluntary. They will feed off the success of associates and their increased income will help grow the individual's confidence and projection for sales. Provide a program that pays service providers for leads received and sold, the supply of service leads will grow quickly. We had a coveted wristwatch with our company logo on the face that was earned through sales achievement.

My sellers were giving their watches to service personnel and a bond was formed. Everyone in both departments brandished that watch, solid leads flowed.

In a service plan the most important action steps are a well-defined training plan that targets product, value to the customer, customer relationships, customer retention and collections of revenue for service rendered. Great customer service doesn't happen by accident, it takes thoughtful, planning, communication, implementation and the right people. Practice customer service as you would sales techniques and learned skills. Use role-playing in training and discuss tips and techniques during meetings. Service people as a whole will resist change but will lean into any technical knowledge you can provide during scheduled meetings.

Recruit every day because Murphy is trolling your team.

**"It does not do to leave a live dragon
out of your calculations,
if you live near one."
J.R.R. Tolkien, writer, poet, philologist, and academic**

LEADERSHIP AND CHARACTER

● ● ● ● ●

By far, the most important ingredient of leadership is your character. You will find that 99% of all the leadership failures in this country in the past 100 years were not failures in competence; they were failures in character...leadership involves morality, and indeed leadership involves integrity, and that is why character is what counts in leadership.
General H. Norman Schwarzkopf,
Commanding Officer Desert Storm

● ● ● ● ●

Throughout history there have been men and women who have used their ability to lead for both good and bad, each is remembered for what they accomplished or for the disaster they caused. What will you do for the people you lead, good or bad?

Management is about the "how and when" events take place, but the "reason why" it happens is called leadership. Leadership is about taking care of the people in your charge. Leadership is given to the leader by the follower who desires to emulate the power of integrity, vision, character and positive focus towards people and relationships. You will be the leader up to the point your people or superiors realize you are not leading. Leaders generate respect by example without fear and leadership elevates people encouraging them to grow in their career and in life. Leaders influence people to accomplish beyond the possible. Leadership is about creating an environment for not only achieving sales and profit plan, but also to achieve human results. There must be a vision encouraging the aspirations of the future that includes a better life for all. When you accept the position of leadership you accept the responsibility for serving others and doing it with a vision for the future. Leadership is not about decision-making or being able to anticipate the next great business pattern or finding business opportunities for that matter, leadership is people centric.

Leaders have a mission, goals, vision and know what they stand for. They lead staff to not only work the plan with high standards but by agreement to excel with the confidence that leads to success. Leadership can see the big picture while working the small picture and to serve others but always with sterling character and always for the welfare of other people. Leadership is courage, character, integrity and the commitment to use responsible authority, but bold enough to take realistic action for excellence without compromise. Be the example people will want to work with, never underestimate the power of your own example.

Character: People are in need of leadership in order to meet their potential and for that reason it is imperative for leadership to have impeccable character traits. A Spartan soldier could lose his spear and sword and still be a citizen, however if he gave up his shield others were at risk in which case, he may lose citizenship or be killed. When management gives up the shield of character there is no leadership and the operation is in danger of failure.

If you are a leader and not merely a manager, you will have to speak up for your team and stand your ground against higher authority. At the same time, you must have the moral courage to address unproductive attitudes and behavior. Where there is no team cohesion everyone fails, a leader will fight for his team.

Communication: In order to guarantee a predictable result everyone must know exactly what to do, how to do it and how to appraise any situation that may require him or her to adapt and overcome. In the same manner team members must communicate with each other to prevent confusion, mistakes and time-wasting duplication of task. What we want is smooth and comfortable conversation from and with our people, to accomplish this management must speak to them. Well-organized and competent staffs that talk to one another will gain the most lasting forms of success and friendship. Use a positive vocabulary because what you say aloud and with your internal voice have a huge influence in how you are perceived by your team. This part is important to you; practice speaking on your digital recorder, do it until you can't get it wrong and your speaking skills will improve quickly.

Some Managers feel that in business meetings they can vent their personal frustrations upon those who can't fight back or defend themselves without escalating the situation or terminating employment. Such a manager had difficulty asserting control over his wife and since control was a big issue for him it led to frustration, and that is being kind. The sales team met as a group every morning to post the board turn in contracts and for the Sales Manager to approve individual sellers planned activity for that day. Occasionally this Manager would arrive at the end of the sales meeting and take over for a three-hour berating session of a sales team that sold more business than some states, and if anyone looked at his watch, he was then be singled out for a furious outburst. Afterwards he was relaxed as easy to talk and work with as anyone could ask. In retrospect, that would have been a good time to ask for a raise in pay. The results of his tantrums were lost productivity for ten sellers for thirty hours on paper, but we all know the actual loss was probably double or triple that, and for zero useful purposes.

In every group there will be one who is weaker or different than others and may become the butt of ugly jokes or bully tactics, do not allow it to happen. Such activity exposes smallness of character and sows' seeds of distrust through the team. Any type of adversarial relationship will prevent unit cohesion and challenge your ability to lead. The other end of that argument is that if you tolerate a bad employee the good employee will leave you. Leadership is about being valuable to the entire team.

General George S. Patton said, "The Army runs on profanity, but it must be eloquent profanity. Sometimes I get carried away with my own eloquence." You do not have the same kind of captive audience as the General and profanity of any kind is out of place no matter how eloquent you believe it may be.

Demand Success: Leadership has the power of success or failure for every company that has ever existed. If you as the leader cannot or do not demand success from everyone, you will never be able to lead others to success. There is no a shortcut to success, and it would not be rewarding if just anyone could do it. Some will want to take shortcuts or the easy way to success that always ends in failure, the more difficult path will always be a better avenue. Leadership must believe that success is possible because success is not an option. Success is the truest form of survival. It is dishonorable for management to put anyone in a position to fail. Inspire others to be their best by being your best.

Success does have some pitfalls to deal with but are really nothing more than a personal challenge that we issue to ourselves. Did you ever notice that people who fail blame everyone except themselves? The successful person has plenty of people to thank for their success but often our heads gets bigger than the moment. Once we have been in the spotlight it can be difficult to step back and be humble, but humble is the next step of your success. Share success and cheer it on but never believe it is about you because you have to do it again and again. If you cannot stay humble and control your pride, there will be a day of reckoning and only yourself to blame.

Motivation: Encouragement and believing in people while guiding them is a very strong motivator for most people. Think of it as lending confidence to those who need a bit of self-assurance. Be relentless in your day-to-day and even your hour-by-hour pursuit of excellence that shapes you and your people by the experience of action. Celebrate small wins as well a large, everyone wants to feel like a winner and it creates a positive atmosphere of recognition and energy, praise is an excellent motivator. Don't be afraid to celebrate, do it early and often. Any form of contempt is the opposite of motivation and kills productivity, always push up, never down.

When you are the leader everyone knows you are in charge, so it follows that when your employees get things done and done well it reflects well on you. Helping others by promoting their success is always better than ineffective self-promotion, promote someone else and do it every day. Take ownership and be of value to the entire team, empower leaders within the team to conduct meetings especially for training issues. Empower the people and they will gain valuable leadership skills that assist you to lead and win. Delegate everything you can, or should, and ask engaging questions that open discussion for interaction with your team to ensure everyone is always on the same page. Do not allow turf conflict, all of the turf belongs to you.

Positive Energy: Successful leaders create a positive and inspiring workplace culture. They set the standard and bring an attitude that motivates their associates to take action. Successful leaders do not focus on protecting turf, they take time to mentor others and expand mutually beneficial relationships. Human behavior will adapt faster to change of rules and routines than you may think, so don't be afraid to change the game. Leadership should never underestimate the power of genuine enthusiasm because it has power, when you feel it, spread it around.

Successful leaders never stop teaching because they are self-motivated to learn all that they can. They use teaching, coaching or mentoring to keep their team knowledgeable and well informed. Requiring staff to conduct training lessons is a great way to improve overall knowledge.

Popularity: No one wants to be unpopular because all of the connotations are negative but in the business arena you must be guarded as to what level of association you allow out of or into your professional space. There must always be a division between you and your staff because familiarity breeds contempt. Do not be aloof but never allow yourself to be valued by your popularity because you cannot lead people you associate with on a social level.

Work: Your employment is an agreement you have with your employer that may have purpose for you and perhaps sharing a vision or values with the employer. For some of us working is easier than relaxing but that creates some unhealthy trade off and offers few if any positive options for family and recreation needed for both mind and body.

Believe this, there is a difference between enjoying work and enjoying yourself. It is okay to enjoy your work, not for the sake of power but for a meaningful and purposeful impact that creates a positive atmosphere where others can enjoy their work. But if work is your life you are failing at life and work.

Discipline: Is all about being in control with fair and equal treatment for all in an organized and efficient way, setting and achieving daily/weekly/ monthly/annual objectives. It's also about having a game plan, being in charge of your life and understanding the wants and needs of the team.

Self- Discipline: If you lack self-discipline and are satisfied with, "I have always been this way," there is trouble on the horizon for you. No one succeeds in life or business without self-discipline. Some people are born with the natural qualities of self-discipline and others of us have to make a decision, most successful people have earned success through hard work, training, support and self-development.

You have the power to develop whatever disciplines you deem desirable and/or necessary for your success in business and in life. It may be easy, or it may require more time, conscious thought and active determination. Every act of self-discipline strengthens and reinforces your other disciplines, you will actually become what you are determined to be. Coincidentally, as your self-disciplines come under control your self-confidence will build strength in you and you will like and respect yourself in new ways. You will find yourself being more confident and optimistic, plus you will succeed at higher levels in everything you attempt.

Mimic: It is smart business to adopt and adapt to how successful people perform in sales or manage their business in order to improve your own performance. But it is a mistake to copy another person because it is impossible to combine the numerous differences of two distinctly different individuals. The results of duplicating another person's actions are frustration and failure. Imagine the Craftsman you can become by being the individual that you are.

Winners: Winners never waste critical time and motion doing what is unproductive to the plan, instead they do meaningful work. Winners feed on creativity, challenge themselves and protect their focus. Winners are generous to others with wealth and experience, always offering a helping hand. Winners never harbor grudges or live with regrets. Trust is built on evidence of many kinds, but relationships are built on trust. Winners invest in relationships.

Losers: Expressing anger towards an employee will lower your position in the eyes of all employees. Create an abusive, manipulative and intolerant atmosphere and the team will turn against you. Losers never apologize for their mistakes. Losers pretend to care about others more than they truly do. Losers refuse to delegate responsibilities and blame others for their failures. Losers allow or create chaos. Losers are emotional or negative in actions and gestures. Losers will fail to upgrade the team even while knowing they are on the road to disaster.

Sports analogies are useful to make a point and there are no better couches to use for this than Paul "Bear" Bryant and Nick Saban because each have a remarkable history of winning seasons. I am by the way a Tennessee fan.

> *"If anything goes bad, I did it. If anything goes semi-good, we did it. If anything goes really good, then you did it. That is all it takes to get people to win football games for you." Paul "Bear" Bryant, Alabama football coach*

> **"If you aren't coaching it you are letting it happen."** *Nick Saban Alabama football coach*

> *"We create a standard for how we want to do things, and everybody's got to buy in to that standard or you really can't have any team chemistry. Mediocre people don't like high achievers and high achievers don't like mediocre people." Nick Saban Alabama football coach*

HIRING WINNERS

• • • • •

"If you pick the right people and give them the opportunity to spread their wings and put compensation as a carrier behind it you almost don't have to manage them.
Jack Welch, American, Business Executive

• • • • •

Hiring and sometimes having to terminate an employee is the most difficult part of management for most of us. There are many things that can go wrong when you are the leader but the most damaging by far is poor hiring decisions. Some leaders fear that by hiring a winner they will put themselves at a risk for this strong person to eventually take their job. Not true, the leader who can hire and manage strong people will always have a job. As a leader you know that results are tied to the team you lead and the stronger your team the better you ensure team momentum. So why not recruit and hire the very best you can find? Strong leaders hire strong people. Weak leaders hire weak people who make the leader look weaker, it is as simple as that. If someone tells you that they want your job, the response is to smile and say, "you can't have my job, but I will help you to get one just like mine." Positive reinforcement always works in a positive way.

I hate failure; I find failure to be totally and completely abhorrent. So, when I had to terminate an employee, with the exception of a policy violation where I had no choice, it was a failure on my part for how I hired, trained, supported or managed. I am guilty of keeping people longer than I should have but my rule for terminating anyone's employment was simple. When I cared more about that person's family

115

survival than the employee, they had to go. Recruiting and hiring is neither a good nor bad experience, but it is a learning experience.

The subject matter of interest here is the process used to hire high performance salespeople, but the process is similar for all departments and all venues. The most sought-after seller is the elusive "high charisma natural salesman." Caution, adhere to the rules of interview or that candidate will take over the interview. If you hire the charismatic applicant be certain that the work ethic matches the charisma, or you will end up working for them, without being paid. The natural salesperson does exist but beware because they are almost exclusively politicians, TV preachers or that guy who from youth was told he could sell ice in the Arctic. Anyone of which is more than willing to take your money and expect you to be grateful that they did. The exception is the guy who had to move to the Arctic because he never learned when to stop talking and bought back the sale before it was closed, he was probably still talking when the bears ate him. Teams are built with average people who are trained and supported and that is your job in a nutshell.

The most important traits to look for in sales professionals are the ability to form genuine close relationships with prospects and the only way to learn whether or not they have these traits is to spend quality interview time with them. Good relationships with customers and prospects turn into loyalty and loyalty turns into repeat business and referrals. These sales professionals prove to be an invaluable addition to any sales team. People with a high energy level, gestures, expressions and tone, among other things are the highest achievers and the quickest thinkers. Successful salespeople have more energy and a more positive attitude towards work and life. They talk but listen and spend more time chatting with prospects and drawing them out. Their positive attitude truly will make a difference with customers and members of the sales team. Each new hire you make will change the environment and personality of the sales team; make sure the change is a positive.

When you have an open sales position, and you will, don't make the mistake of giving insufficient due diligence in the recruiting process because hiring is a high stakes game. Give yourself the best chance of building a winning sales team by hiring winners for your team and not some other company's castoff's. This part is very important to you, when you are interviewing, the prospect is selling their desire to work at your company. If they are professional salespeople, they are reading you and adapting their presentation to what they read. Hold your cards close and maintain control until you have enough information to make a hire that will compliment you. The more you investigate the less you have to invest.

Plan the search to attract well-qualified candidates with a compelling company story. Attracting qualified candidates can be accomplished internally or externally. You may have internal candidates who are qualified for the position. My preference by experience was not to target competing industries and companies for candidates, I did not like to un-train bad habits. A common mistake involves not evaluating enough candidates. Also, realize that depending on the position you may need to screen between 50 to 100 applicants, so be prepared to do your homework. I have placed ads in the employment section only to have a mob of people swamp my office. If I did my job properly some of those people had to wait for hours before I could see them and that was extremely poor planning on my part. So, I began to take the initial interview by phone. I used a designated line for inbound calls and used a form of my design but similar to our application form to fill in as we talked. There are a number of benefits involved in this process. I could speak comfortably at length with prospects of interest and I could listen to how well the prospect spoke and communicated, which is of great interest to me while I gathered information. It will be very long days to speak to all applicants, some early and some late.

Interview steps

Introduction, your name and job title
Overview of interview
State the job title and job description being interviewed for
Obtain information - Tell me about you
Review education history - Review job history
Close or Schedule an in-person interview
Call references and past employers

TELEPHONE INTERVIEW

DATE___ POSITION ___ 1ST INTERVIEW ___ 2ND INTERVIEW___

NAME_____ PHONE _____ CELL _____

CITY _____ HOW LONG _____ MOVED FROM _____

MILITARY-----BRANCH_____ YEARS _____ JOB _____

VEHICLES OWNED _____

MOVING VIOLATIONS #_____ TYPE _____ AT FAULT #_____

VALID TN DR LICENSE YES NO   D. U. I. CONVICTIONS   YES NO
DRIVE STRAIGHT SHIFT. YES NO   FELONY CONVICTION YES NO
LIABILITY INSURANCE. YES NO   CURRENTLY EMPLOYED YES NO
PRE-EMP DRUG TEST   YES NO   TIME OUT OF WORK _____

EMPLOYER_____ HOW LONG _____

DUTIES _____ EARNINGS _____

REASON FOR LEAVING _____

EMPLOYER _____ HOW LONG _____

DUTIES _____ EARNINGS _____

REASON FOR LEAVING _____

EMPLOYER _____ HOW LONG _____

DUTIES _____ EARNINGS _____

REASON FOR LEAVING _____

TELL ME ABOUT YOURSELF_____

_____

_____

_____

OBSERVATIONS _____

_____

_____

_____

Interviewing candidates. The interview process is the most common method of candidate selection method and is also the least reliable. Interviews rarely reflect real-life situations and don't show the candidate's true patterns of behavior. "Tell me about yourself" will bring out quick and telling responses about family life and personality traits. Some studies have suggested that as much as 80 percent of hiring decisions are made in the first 10 minutes of an interview. If you do that you are looking for big trouble because it will be the evil twin you have to contend with. Make sure to follow the criteria for candidate selection you developed during your search-planning process. For those candidates who survive the telephone interview schedule an interview in your office. During this interview spend time exploring the candidate's past success and failures, since patterns of success and failure will often indicate future performance. There is no such thing as a detail too small to ask about.

In person interview. I did what I could to relax the candidate; nervous people will hide as much as possible and I wanted the interview to develop as much information as possible, two extremes. I introduced myself and took the candidate to my office and offered coffee, seated them and explained we were here to talk about them and how they may fit in. I pull out the bottom drawer of my desk, propped a foot on it and asked about their favorite football team. I wanted to connect through conversation, and I wanted the prospect to talk to me about what made them enthusiastic. Cover the information you have on the telephone interview asking questions that require explanation while looking for contradicting statements. Discuss references but remember that personal references are always biased. Make it clear you intend to speak with past reporting managers as to the specifics of their duties, achievements and ability to work internally with peers. A good time to say this is before you ask, "is there anything else I should know or that you would like me to tell me." Cautious responses can be a red flag, what isn't said is often more telling than what is said.

Schedule a second interview in your office especially if other management will be involved in training and or supervision. Make that interview about the company, how this person could fit in and introduce to other sales staff and perhaps ride along with a trusted team member. If we want this candidate, we want him or her to want to be with us.

If your candidate is a believed to be or can be a high-performance seller, he or she may receive a counteroffer from the current employer. By determining the candidate's motivation, you will have a higher probability of closing your sale. A salary bidding war is counterproductive for your ability to manage this person and will create a negative in the sales team. I want the person who wants to be on my team.

Attributes of winners - losers and a few questions:

- I don't have to make a lot of money, but I want to.
- A commitment to God, family and work in that order.
- A sense of modesty.
- Achievement that has come from being ruthless with him or herself but not with others.
- Social media is informative but so are phone answering messages and how the person answers a phone when they don't know it is a career call. What does the email address tell you about the applicant?
- Personal hygiene counts. Smelling of cigarette smoke, having body odor or garlic and onions will be offensive to staff and prospects. What's for lunch?
- Arriving super-early or late for an interview is a serious caution flag.
- Beware of people who give "magic bullet" answers.
- Manners count, good manners count more. When you call a new prospect, do you thank the executive assistant, receptionist or gatekeeper even if you are not connected with that person?
- Physical appearance matters, can this person do the job, is he or she two different from the customer base to connect in a positive way? This is not about race or gender, but it could be about facial tattoos as an example.
- Do you include the word please when asking for help?

- Do you thank your boss for his or her feedback and guidance?
- Self-Discipline, who is in control?

Internet sites offer pre-screened applicants and the commercials sound as if when you click on that a magical person will appear. They will not, there is a process you must follow because hiring is the most important part of your job and perhaps your career. For those who may find the preceding process too cumbersome, re-read the back cover of this publication.

"Hiring is a form of investing. You have to do your research and make sure you're spending your resources in the right place."
Warren Edward Buffett, Chairman and CEO of Berkshire Hathaway

TRAINING & RETENTION

• • • • •

*"We are what we repeatedly do. Excellence
then, is not and act, but a habit."*
Aristotle, Ancient Greek Teacher &Philosopher

• • • • •

Most new seller training will cover the basics of the products that are to be sold and perhaps a little sales training, then the seller is sent out to find success or to find failure. Most fail, because they are unprepared for success. When we were in school, we learned how to be book smart and perhaps how some things work but we did not learn how to sell. Salespeople must be trained and supported if they are to be successful at their primary task of securing new revenue. Training builds unit integrity, weeds out bad attitudes, lowers customer complaints, and increases leads and referrals. Training breeds confidence and competence obediently follows. Managing the resulting retention of successful employees is the easiest part of any supervisor's job description.

Experience does not always come with longevity; we all know someone who has been in their job for many years, but their knowledge and performance are stagnant. Coaching requires a proactive influence and higher activity levels. Coaching is about helping people change or improve their professional skills level. It can be about business practice changes to sharpen skills and sometimes it may require a change of conduct. Coaching is a process that brings results; focus on the process not on the end result.

No matter what the job title the instructor holds he/she must be a good operator, but a good operator may not be a good instructor. The instructor must have the appropriate patience and communication skills to communicate on the student's level if you are to build a Craftsman. The Instructor will need to understand and be able to define the difference between an objection and a stall, what and how to use a hidden command, how to find the prospects wants and needs, create value and how to get referrals without asking. Beware of using existing sales staff to assist training if they are lead dependent. A lead dependent seller will often times discourage the new employee by telling them their likelihood of earning a living in that position is impossible.

The 4 steps of training are the foundation that training stands upon.

Orientation – Tell them what will be discussed and expected results to be achieved.

Demonstration – Show how each step is perfectly performed.

Observation – Observe and note areas to be discussed during evaluation.

Evaluation – Discuss the task, what was done well and what was not and how to improve in a time frame.

Repeat at a higher activity level

SALES FORMULA:

- Create Confidence with warm up conversation
- Define the Problem what are the prospects wants and needs
- Offer the Solution, Acme, Inc. can fulfill the wants and needs and this is how Qualify Your Company, Acme, Inc. is the best choice to fill your wants and needs because
- Describe the Benefits Warranty and trouble-free relationship
- Close the Sale Ask for the money, sign right here I will get the work scheduled.

How do we measure the immeasurable, with a digital recorder of course? Everything can be practiced on your digital or video recorder. Leave yourself a short voicemail that you would want someone to hear if they were leaving it for you. Practice your presentation, practice overcoming stalls and objections, practice closing, practice prospecting, practice warm up, better than that practice telling a special someone you love them. Perfect presentation practice makes perfect sales presentations and role-playing will sharpen selling skills for the group, record it and play it back for evaluation. Role-playing can be great fun and constructive when done without ridicule.

The seller must have a plan and be prepared to present at many different levels and there is no better way to prepare than with a digital or video recorder. You will expose your discomfort with the content of your presentation, the use of too many filler words and disorderly transitions, "you know". You can always do this thing with your wife or a special person, but you can bet they will tell you how good it was even if they have no clue what you said. You are the only one who will know when it is right and ready for public use.

Under no circumstance record presentations of actual conversations with your prospect. It may be illegal if the prospect is unaware and you are certain to lose the sale and perhaps the interview if you ask for permission

Expect success from those you train and tell them you expect success, it is very satisfying to see. Tell them to trust and believe in their training and to exercise their faith.

References:

Why Talent Walks Out the Door www.skillsoft.com
Train the Trainer www.corporaterainingmatterials.com
Dale Carnegie Effective Speaking and Human relations

"Train people well enough so they can leave,
treat them well enough so they don't want to."
Richard Branson, British businessman and investor

ASSOCIATE RELATIONS

● ● ● ● ●

"Those who work well with others survive" Author Unknown

● ● ● ● ●

If all we needed to do was flip a switch to turn on our robots, running a business would be easy, but we must manage people which is not always easy. And the bigger the company the smaller the likelihood that everyone will be easy to supervise or that they will get along with one another. You can always terminate someone who is team resistant but good talent is hard to find. So, it's worth the effort to help make a difficult personality work more effectively with you and other associates. When faced with a problem personality, most of us will do one of two things. We confront the person head-on, which will usually make the situation worse, or we avoid dealing with him or her which allows the problem to worsen. As the leader the only satisfactory resolution you can afford is a positive resolution. Communicating in a calm manner doesn't mean you can't be firm, you are the boss, but do not be reactive and don't rigidly lay down the law. We are equally responsible for our actions and our reactions, act but do not react. Why not invite that person into your office or meet for coffee and discuss the issues, you may be amazed at what you learn? You are a Sales Manager; here is where you can use your skills to help the troublesome employee use their own energies in ways that will benefit themselves, their co-workers and your company. But remember, it is never "not personal" when another person is involved or affected it will be personal. So, don't be too surprised if this person challenges you, people typically react when their buttons are pushed, now it's personal. If that happens, take a break, breathe, and center yourself and control the situation, insecurity is loud, but confidence is calm. Then respond calmly and firmly to resolve an issue rather than get caught up in a circular logic discussion. You must be the role model for those around you and you have the higher ground, stay above the fight.

With a word of caution, this part is very important to you: when interviewing a disruptive employee, it is a good idea to have a manager or supervisor to witness, use a video recorder or digitally record the proceedings. The employee may object but I would rather handle that objection than to having my reputation stained before the people I work for much less defend myself in a court of law. Turn the recorder on before the meeting starts and do not turn it off until the employee has left your presence. Be sure to advise the employee that the meeting is being recorded and ask him or her to clearly verify that they are aware of the recording. Date and time stamp the meeting introducing all parties present and their acknowledgement of and acceptance of the recording, then state the purpose for the meeting and begin. This part is very important to you, people will act in predictable ways and with predictable behavior, if you carefully observe them and take note of their patterns of behavior you will be able to recognize the predictable end.

True story: The Seller was a sales board leader who caused a toxic atmosphere in his salesroom. Despised by his associates he was arrogant, scheming, disruptive, dishonest, self-centered, an arm twisting closer and at the same time somehow religious. The situation went unchecked because the manager didn't talk to employees he did not like. The predictive result was that when it came to a head the manager lost his temper and the termination was on the verge of physical violence. The moral is that good behavior with reward is repeated behavior while as in this case bad behavior rewarded by negligence became worse behavior. The terminated employee claimed to be abused and discriminated against in letters and phone calls to Corporate and to the Region Manager. Less troublesome employees had resigned, and sales revenues were flat, it was shortly after that I became Sales Manager in that office. Four years had passed with the office becoming a major revenue source for the company, selling more business than the two major cities in our state. I had a very strong sales team who were among the highest paid commissioned sellers in the company when, yep, you guessed it. After having self-counseled and prayed about it he used his considerable sale acumen to convince two layers above me that he was now a good fit and that he should be reinstated. It was firmly but politely suggested that I should speak with him and bring him into the sales team. I responded that he was a known commodity to be avoided and as many reasons as I could think of not to hire him, to no avail. The greed for revenue beyond logical boundaries has caused the downfall of uncountable businesses. I left it with he will have to call me for an appoint to interview, he did. Life offers many traps to make you fail unless you take control. The appointment was set at a local coffee shop and he was to bring along a pen and a notebook. He did not, what kind of salesman doesn't have a pen? There was a newspaper nearby so I had him write down all of the poor character choices he had made and could not ever commit again. He was on a strict line of discipline and was going to be treated like any other new employee including the training regimen. Further he was not allowed to hang any of his past awards or plaques in the sales room, he must start fresh. He was required to keep his handwritten newspaper notes in his wallet and when he acted out I had him retrieve the note and read the entire list out loud, in private of course. He was severely out classed in the sales room and never again a leader on the sale board although he had more leads than he had ever had before. Less than a year had past when he became sullen and angry, he was his old self once more, the perfect storm of discontent and destruction. I gave him three carefully worded written reprimands and copied to HR and Management; I then terminated his employment. Yep, you guessed it, he launched an attack on Corporate and the Region Manager verbatim to his prior termination. I took control of what I knew was going to be a negative situation and refused to allow it to affect my business, consequently no one ever discussed specific hires with me again.

This part is very important to you, every new hire and every termination will change the environment and the personality of the sales team either for better or for worse, make sure it is for the better.

The environment we work in is stronger than our will power. The environment you provide will either inspire people to generate revenue or kill their will to produce. It will facilitate your success, or it will detract from it. It will energize the sales team, or it will drain them. The good news is that you have a lot of control over the sales room environment.

In a new operation or office, it is a good idea to get the sales team engaged and remove clutter, get files organized, paint the walls and re-decorate the sales room. A positive environment will elevate feelings and behaviors and is especially important on days that aren't going well. Would you rather have a salesperson whose day has just fallen apart working in a comfortable office environment that has a positive impact or at home comfortable in a recliner?

SEX AND THE OFFICE: In a moment of foolish behavior, you may think that remarks of a sexual nature are funny, but you can bet what will be your last paycheck that someone else is deeply offended. Some people think that intrusive questions regarding someone's sex life, unwanted flirtation, touching or what may be described as "being playful" is amusing, but those laughing with you are taking notes. You can make jokes that you think are funny, after all doesn't everyone want to be popular even admired for their wit, but others hear a crude form of demeaning harassment, or even worse for you a sexual assault claim. The terminated employee gets no admiration for their wit from their employer or their employees and certainly not from a spouse, but you can ruin your life and career. Claims of being misinterpreted will fall on deaf ears because once charged you are a liability, you are guilty until proven innocent but that will never happen.

No one, management or otherwise survives a sexual harassment claim, it happens to the innocent as well as the guilty. Some people are victims, and some people are liars, but the publicity, legal cost and potential payout require someone to be terminated from their employment. Even if the offender isn't terminated the stain on his/her character and career is indelible and it will headline your résumé for your continued work life. It doesn't matter how popular you are with your bosses, or how talented or productive you are, once accused of sexual harassment you are a liability. That means that because of your actions a substantial amount of money is on the table, you are the reason and therefore you are expendable.

Protect yourself and do not allow your office atmosphere to have any type of sexual overtones and treat everyone with dignity and the same respect you would want shown to a loved one.

OFFICE POLITICS: No matter where you work or what you do, there's one thing every professional must deal with in the workplace and that is office politics. Most people don't like office politics but if that is the environment you allow; you can bet they will all join in and you are an inviting target. Some join in a passive manner but others are totally committed, whatever level you allow will destroy morale and productivity for your office. In its extreme office politics can and has developed into physical violence and death. How you handle office politics can make or break your professional career prospects, but handling the situation is not a complex task. A commonsense approach, courtesy and compromise from a position of strength can keep the players in line without getting you mired in political pitfalls. Often the office politicians are influential and are likely to be high profile individuals. I delighted in reminding my politicians not to play with Dragons saying, "Meddle not in the affairs of Dragons, for they find you crunchy and tasty with ketchup".

FAILURE TO PRODUCE OR COMPLY: General Sun Tsu in the Art of War said, "if the orders are unclear it is the fault of the General but if the orders are clear it is the fault of the subordinate." In order to execute the employee must know what is expected and how to achieve results. Hiring well is only part of the equation, a large part for sure, but support through training, mentoring and supervision are the methods used for insuring employee success. Training should be on going and at regular intervals. Training is a great teacher for the teacher, so why not assign employees to conduct an occasional training meeting, assisted and supervised of course. What can be done for the employee who just doesn't produce or comply? Termination is an option, but recruiting is time consuming, expensive and one of our own is involved, therefore it should be the last step to take. What do you know about this employee, is there trouble at home, a divorce, an addiction or alcohol problem, has someone close died or have they simply lost interest in the company's mission? Has he/she been counseled, can this employee be motivated and if so, what have you done to motivate this employee? A review of documentation and all of these questions must be answered before termination should become an option. An employee who fails to comply is a challenge but if the supervisor has done his/her part then the employee is the only one who can solve the problem.

THE GOSSIP: Stay away from the gossip and never say anything you don't want everyone to know, unless you do want everyone to know.

THE SABOTEUR: He or she carries that proverbial knife to back stab any and all that he/she can't control. This is the one who leads the parking lot meeting after your meeting and his version challenges yours and their message is negative to yours, so join his meeting and document. Somehow and in some way the saboteur will blame others for real or imagined offenses. For the saboteur, making those offenders look bad or in some way ending their employment while being the beacon of purity is the end game. Don't be surprised if your saboteur is closely aligned with an executive and serves as his eyes and ears. Measure your words and be thoughtful as to how you use them because words have meaning and meaning matter, so be clear with your statements. Thinking and listening are free if you do a lot of it, document everything.

FRENEMIES: The Godfather said, "Keep your friends close and your enemies closer." Workplace relationships are very common and can become true lifelong friendships. They can also get you, fired, or divorced and cause a host of problems you did not see coming. There will always be someone ready to take full credit for your achievements, even though this person is your friend. Recognizing someone who has an eye on your job can seem like work in itself and it is disappointing when it happens. Management in today's workplace often seems cold and distant and with good reason. Should the workplace friend have behavior issues it is doubly difficult to discipline or terminate them. Before taking any steps in this situation you must look at your own behavior, did your actions open the door for their behavior is a good place to start? If your behavior is equally poor an attempt to discipline will only make an enemy. Professional relationships must be handled with care but not overly guarded, you are in charge of what happens good or bad.

THE REGAL: This person is interested in themselves and little more, they are loaded with trouble and will cause countless headaches for you. They will interview well and have all of the right answers, but it will be the evil twin who comes to work when hired. They will have a history of job changes, avoid hiring them no matter how well they interview. If you inherit one of these people document events until you can exit them from your team. The Regal is confident and easy to talk to and wants to be the center of attention in every situation. They may dress with more jewelry, nicer accessories or dress to be noticed. They are gossips with a penchant for stretching the truth if not outright lying. You will find them in the middle of every office crisis that they may have created but will never accept responsibility for their actions. They will also tell you how to do your job as though you work for them. The Regal will provoke you until action on your part is required and then become the victim. Document, document and document because they will.

DRAMA AND NEGATIVITY IN THE OFFICE: For some people drama is their life's blood and no one is off limits. They create wars and infighting over just about everything but most especially their coveted turf and the success of their associates. For them the break room, coffee area or the water cooler are their domain to create collaborative trouble for others and drain the energy of your sales team. Because drama is like stirring the poop pot management especially executives attempt to ignore the drama, or they handle it so badly that the problem gets bigger and harder to deal with. Those people are about their own interest with no interest in the team or you and that is the root of deliberate misunderstandings. Negative people have a problem for every solution, find a way to ease them out of the operation.

TROUBE AT HOME: You can expect that at least half of your employees will experience problems in their personal lives with their children, spouse or a parent. Those with personal challenges will experience trouble concentrating, their production will fall off, they will miss meetings, appointments and be absent from work. Make no mistake, personal problems for a staff member is a problem for you and it is a serious challenge to deal with. Employees have come to my office, sometimes in tears, and told me their deepest secrets and troubles. It is best to take the compassionate and fair approach; I would always take a chair beside that employee and listen to the end but do not ever touch the employee no matter how sympathetic you may be. You can and should ask if the company is contributing to this stressful situation and make reasonable adjustments where possible. Ask your employee what you can do to help, making sure you are not part of the problem. Asking personal questions will make the situation worse for you, do not do it. Other employees will take note of how you treat a struggling associate and will likely be more open to discuss personal issues with you but never involve yourself into their lives, be the example in their lives. If the associate needs counseling or drug or alcohol abuse, most companies will have some resources to provide.

There are excellent classes and books written to help you learn to deal with associate relations, most will tell you how to carve out any cancers with a scalpel. When I was faced this drama in my office, I tried to handle it more decisively and if necessary, with the sword. I held regular office meetings alongside daily and weekly gatherings by department, so I knew who and what was and was not working in my office. Meetings are an excellent opportunity to explain that everyone is there at the pleasure of the company and that each of them has a production schedule to complete and that schedule does not include time for gossip and drama. Pointing to greater production can be an attention getter. I was transferred to an office that was well known to be run by inmates who ignored the chain of command and would fearlessly call upon middle management in person and by phone to report any grievance. During the introduction I made a point of covering chain of command. I advised that if anyone found themselves unhappy with me or with policy that could not be settled in my office, that I would make a call to the next level to schedule a meeting for both of us. However, anyone who disregarded the chain of command would be terminated without further review. The main culprits were two in the service department and the office bookkeeper. I promoted one to Service Manager and moved the other to sales and launched my business plan. Now the conspirators are adversaries and the increase in revenue took gossip time away from the bookkeeper, everyone made more money.

THIS PART IS VERY IMPORTANT TO YOU: If you don't already have a business plan put one together and roll it out in an office meeting, with food and beverage, detailing numbers and actions by department. Ask your staff to buy in and refer to their copy often, now everyone has a mutually desirable goal as well as a reason to support team members. Discipline, and always focusing on the positive is the key to success when managing people, if you don't take control the inmates will. Employees who trust management will work faster and with less stress, be trustworthy.

"When there is no consequence for poor work ethic,
and no reward for good ethic, there is no motivation".
John David Roberts, NFL Coach

EMPLOYEE PERFORMANCE EVALUATIONS

• • • • •

Feedback is important to people. We all want
to know how well we're doing.
That's why it is essential for an effective performance review
system to provide ongoing feedback.
Kenneth H. Blanchard, Author of the One Minute Manager

• • • • •

Most employees believe performance evaluations are a waste of time or even punishment and with good cause. Most appraisals are conducted by an untrained and poorly prepared supervisor who may evaluate by subjective opinion while overlooking objective data. You know that is true because it has happened to you. When the supervisor isn't fully aware of how to proceed in a comprehensive process of evaluation the employee will not know how they were evaluated nor will they know the end-to-end process of the performance review. So, the employee is left to question, "where do I fit in."

There are some excellent reasons for management to have a dedicated partnership with employees through employee evaluations and an open exchange of feedback.

Improving overall team performance: Unit improvement and job security are the most important reasons for you to have a performance evaluation system. It encourages coaching and mentoring activity that will create increased morale for the team and skill development for management. A system of regular performance review will allow management to communicate performance expectations to every member of the team and assess exactly how well each person is doing. When everyone is aware of their performance expectations and how they are performing against expectations, excellence will become the norm.

Providing Legal Defensibility: Virtually all personnel decisions ranging from denial of a promotion, termination, or transfer to a different department or office can be subjected to legal scrutiny. Documentation is legal evidence that you actively involved the employee in the evaluation, recognition or promotion process without discrimination. Documentation is proof that management provided clear explanations of what the company expects from the employee in their job performance. If you are challenged, you must be able to demonstrate that decisions made were not based on the individual's protected status. Documentation of employee performance appraisals greatly facilitates legal defensibility when a complaint about discrimination is made. No matter that you don't like to do it, you must document everything.

Most employees will respect the manager who communicates with them but who holds them accountable for high standards of operation and discipline. But employees will hate the manager who holds them to arbitrary expectations without communicating with them or listening to them. Court cost is always greater than the air it takes to communicate with people.

Validating Hiring Decisions: Are you hiring winners, or is it the evil twin who reports for work? Only when the performance of new hires is evaluated can the management know whether or not you are hiring the right people. You must regularly assess your bench strength to make sure you have talent and that it is in the right place. Performance evaluations will give management the tools they need to make sure they have the talent required to be an industry leader.

Goals Setting: Goal setting by management and by employee has consistently proven to raise standards and generate superior performance at all levels. A strong performance evaluation process will ensure that every member of the organization sets and achieves effective goals.

Training and Development: If you have transferred between departments or offices, you will have met a tenured employee who has never progressed beyond basic training, has never been evaluated much less being exposed to goal setting. Longevity does not equal training or skill advancement. But the employee evaluation coupled with development plans and good business decisions about skills and competencies development will cause a greater contribution to the company. As a result, the opportunity for promotion is increased and the odds of layoff are lower.

Promotion and Compensation: Determining compensation increases and preparedness for new role responsibility cannot be fairly established without an evaluation system. Some will move into management roles or team leader roles, but they must be prepared for that responsibility and have the requisite skill set to do the job. If the promoting supervisor desires to achieve a higher position it is smart business to be sure those who represent you are competent.

Poor Performers: Not everyone will meet company standards, but the density can be limited and improved with counseling, coaching, mentoring, training and increased engagement by management and the employee. Performance evaluations force management to confront those whose performance does not meet company expectations on a professional level. Words have power that can lift someone up or knock them down, a simple sentence can be profound enough to build or destroy. The platform for both the employee and the supervisor is to attain common ground on which both believe the process is a quality experience.

Developing an Inclusive Performance Culture

What is a performance evaluation? Performance Evaluation is defined as a formal and productive procedure to measure an employee's work results based on their job responsibilities. It is used to gauge the amount of value added by an employee in terms of productivity in comparison to company standards and the overall return on investment the employee brings to the company. In a different term, job security for everyone.

What is the purpose of a performance evaluation? The primary purpose for performance evaluations is to improve the way a team or company functions and to achieve higher levels of revenue capture and customer satisfaction leading to customer retention and greater profits. To establish "win-win" communications between the company and the employee by focusing on employee performance and development. To provide feedback on the employee's career path while building on strengths and providing leadership for areas that require improvement with training and support to reach performance goals. The performance evaluation is also used to grade an employee for the retention of talent, promotion to greater responsibility and for suitable compensation management. There will of course be negative evaluations concluding in termination of employment.

Documentation: You must document each area of the employee job description because you can't assess that which you have not measured. Have data on hand that is collected from the last evaluation.

Objectives & Goals: The objective is to ensure that an employee can reach and surpass performance and earnings expectations. To do that will require goals setting that is not totally arbitrary but gives the employee input, buy in and a strong desire to engage in the process.

Not all of your employees have clear goals that optimize the benefits of an evaluation. Without goal setting and clear objectives your appraisals will become a process of simply going through the motions.

Measuring Performance: Measuring performance that is expressed in numeric terms, sales, service, cost, quantity, quality and attendance are relatively easy to do. Most evaluations are derived from a numerical score based on productivity goals. It is a good system because it is objective and the numbers speak for themselves, plus methods of improvement are clearly defined.

Performance Evaluation Action Steps

- Gather performance and development information both positive and negative taken from documented evidence and prepare the report with integrity. Divide the positives and negatives into two categories, you want the employee to be better able to see a broader picture. Keep the feedback constructive and avoid opinions.
- Communicate performance standards, job expectations and prepare the employee to give and receive information with an open mind and in a comfortable environment. Be candid and consistent when stating facts from documented evidence to the employee. Performance appraisal is not the time to reprimand an employee, but it is a good time counsel and plan for an improved team member. Counseling in itself is a two-way process working with an employee and to understand the cause of the unsatisfactory quality and quantity of work.
- Explain the affect pro or con and assess the data together. Both supervisor and employee must be mutually engaged in the process for a productive conclusion.
- Use assessments to develop and assign an agreed upon but clearly deliverable objective with a reasonable due date and document the evolution of the assigned projects against the current employee's productivity.
- State the expected results of agreed upon action and develop any additional training or ongoing support that is required.
- Document with accuracy each step.
- Review all documentation, acquire signatures, time stamp and date signed on all pages of the evaluation.

- Conclude with positive energy.
- The employee may wish to write a response to the review in the space indicated in the form, or to attach a lengthier response to it. Once this is complete, the employee and the supervisor both sign it.

"Done right, a performance review is one of the best opportunities to encourage and support high performers and constructively improve your middle- and lower-tier workers."
Kathryn Minshew, American Entrepreneur, CEO of The Muse

SUMMARY

• • • • •

The purpose for negotiating is to replace negative problems with positive solutions.

The purpose for prospecting is to make new friends who will become customers and prevent us from living in poverty.

The purpose for preparation is to have a strong mental and physical advantage in the marketplace.

The purpose for building a firm relationship is because people never forget how you make them feel.

The purpose for taking control is to present yourself as a professional and guide the prospect through the sales process to a successful close.

The purpose for warmup, no matter how long it takes, is to establish common ground and build a solid relationship with the prospect.

The purpose for wants and needs is to define the problem and establish that you have the product or service the prospect needs or desires and deserves.

The purpose for the presentation is to transfer belief and assurance that you are the most logical person with whom to do business.

The purpose for trial close questions is to acquire the prospects opinion (conviction) that is also a commitment to buy before leaving one segment and leading into the next presentation segment.

The purpose for a chain of convictions is to build a since of urgency through positive opinions and commitments that produce leverage and lead to a clean close.

The purpose for the close is to end negotiations, acquire a signed contract, a check or finance agreement and at least one referral.

The purpose for referrals is to spend less time on the phone and more time selling and earning.

The purpose for cool down is to solidify the relationship and overcome buyer's remorse.

The purpose for repetitively stating "this part is important to you, use any electronic device and practice until you can't get it wrong" is because doing so is vital to your economic success.

HOMEWORK – IT IS
NOT OPTIONAL

● ● ● ● ●

"Everyone talks about finding their voice, do your homework
and your voice will find you."
Bradford Marsalis, American band leader

● ● ● ● ●

How to Stop Worrying and Start Living – Dale Carnegie

Finding Your Element – Ken Robinson

Emotional Intelligence – Daniel Coleman

Seasons of Life – Jim Rohn, Ronald L. Reynolds

Midas Touch - Robert Kiyosaki

The Law of Success - Napolean Hill

7 Strategies for Wealth & Happiness – Jim Rohn

The Power of Ambition – Jim Rohn

Personal Styles and Effective Performance - D.W. Merrill & R.H. Reid

Applications in Non-Verbal Communications - Ronald E. Riggio &
Robert S. Feldman

Body Language – David Cohen

How to Read Customers Accurately - Ken Dooley

How to Listen and Double Your Influence with Others - *Brian Tracy*

The Birth Order Book - Dr. Kevin Leman

The 7 Habits of Highly Effective People - Stephen R. Covey

I Wish I'd Said That! How to Talk Your Way Out of Trouble and Into Success - Linda McCallister

D.I.S.C. Personality Test - William Moulton Marston, Phycologist

Social Styles - David Merrill & Roger Reid

The 4 social styles - Jonathan Farrington

The Psychology of Selling – Brian Tracy

Secrets of Power Negotiating – Roger Dawson

Getting to Yes – Roger Fisher & William Ury

BE CONFIDENT

ALWAYS ASSUME THE SALE

BE PERSISTENT

FEAR NOTHING

PLAN TO WIN

EXPECT TO WIN

TRUST YOUR TRAINING

SUCCESS BREEDS SUCCESS

TAKE TIME TO HAVE FUN

Lightning Source UK Ltd.
Milton Keynes UK
UKHW041830300421
382942UK00008B/364/J